AF241136

9 781931 013154

THE POMFRET PRAYERBOOK

A Friday Night Service

Compiled by Leigh Ronald Grossman

The Wildside Press

Rockville, Maryland

The Pomfret Prayerbook
A Swordsmith Book
www.swordsmith.com

This book is dedicated to the memory of Rabbi David Honigsberg, whose wisdom remains a constant source of inspiration.

This book is available at quantity discounts for orders of 25 or more. For more information, please contact The Wildsidepress, www.wildsidepress.com or 301-762-1305.

Cover and Interior design by Leigh Grossman
Special thanks to John Betancourt and Kim Lawson

ISBN 1-931013-15-2
ISBN-13 978-1-931013-15-4

Distributed by:
Wildside Press
9710 Traville Gateway Drive #234
Rockville, MD 20850
www.wildsidepress.com

First Wildside Press edition: August 2008

10 9 8 7 6 5 4 3 2 1

INTRODUCTION

The *Pomfret Prayerbook* is designed for occasional use at weddings or Bar and Bat Meetzvot, where it can be given to guests inexpensively. While it can be used for regular weekly services, much of the festival content has been shortened, and extra space has been given to explanations for various prayers. Above all, this book is designed to make the Friday Night service easy to read and sing even for those who are encountering the text for the first time.

Because of the intended audience, much of the material is designed for people who may not be familiar with practices at a Jewish Conservative service, or at any Jewish service at all. While there are notes on when to bow, when to sing, and the like, it's important to know that these practices vary widely from congregation to congregation, and each synagogue or group of worshippers develops its own customs and order of service. So follow the lead of the rabbi and other worshippers, even if it conflicts with the instructions here.

You may hear people pronouncing words differently than those in the transliteration as well. There are two common methods of pronouncing Hebrew (as well as many regional accents) and this book uses the one most prevalent in the United States. But don't be confused of some of the people around you pronounce some *T* sounds as *S* sounds.

The *Pomfret Prayerbook* was first used at the wedding of Leigh Grossman and Rowena Sandoval in Pomfret, Connecticut, on August 8, 2008. The book was created by Leigh Grossman with the guildance and spiritual advice of Alan Turner, leader of Congregation B'nai Shalom in Putnam, Connecticut. Many others provided valuable suggestions and ideas along the way, including Gus Anderson, Lisa Austin, Robin Bogner, Elizabeth Glover, Wendy Goldberg, Amy Goldschlager, Meg Grossman, Marge Guerin, Nancy Hanger, David Lowell, David Norwood, Faye Ringel, Sandy Sadler, Steve Schimmel, Sue and Jordan Stern, David Stern, and countless others. Any mistakes are purely my own. Intern Kim Lawson was responsible for keeping me sane during the final stages of production. And this book would not have been possible at all without the remarkable generosity of John Betancourt of The Wildside Press.

PRONOUNCIATION GUIDE

Because many users of this book won't be familiar with Hebrew, the tranliteration emphasizes ease of use over keeping words together. For instance, the word for Israel is rendered as Yisra eil, to avoid confusion about vowel pronounciation. Hebrew is filled with schwa sounds and pauses that are difficult to render into English, and ease of use is emphasized over perfect pronunciation here. Vowel sounds are always pronounced as follows:

i, ih	as in *kid*
oh	as in *joke*
a, ah	as in *hot*
ei	as in *weigh*
ee	as in *meet*
u	as in *root*
c	is always hard, like k

The two sounds which do not occur in English are rendered as *kh* for the glottal ח and כ, and as *tz* for צ.

NOTES ON THE TRANSLATION

Treatment of gender in a prayerbook is always tricky, particularly given the lack of non-gendered pronouns in the English language. Since God is not gendered, I've used nonspecific gender references except where gender is used metaphorically, such as God's relationship with the Jewish people being like a king to his subjects or the aspect of the divine that is personified as the Sabbath Queen. In order to avoid using gender that isn't specific in Hebrew but is usually translated as *He* in English, I've used the second person You in many places, in order to come closer to what I feel is the intent of the text.

The divine name is rendered as יי in Hebrew, and as *God* in English. Under Jewish customs, because it contains references to the divine, this book must be treated with special respect. If it falls, it should be kissed on the cover, and it cannot be thrown out. If you wish to dispose of it, please donate it to a synagogue or Jewish friend who will know how to do so.

Some of the translations are based on other sources, or adapted and modernized from older prayers. Any translations that are not mine are noted in the text.

WHY DO WE LIGHT SHABBAT CANDLES?

One of the things that we are commanded to do on the Sabbath is to enjoy the Sabbath day and to honor it. This falls under the commandment of "oneg Shabbat," which in English means "to delight in or to take pleasure in the Sabbath."

The prophet Isaiah (58:13) tells the Jewish people that they will be blessed if they honor the Sabbath "and call the Sabbath a delight." Many of the songs that we sing on the Sabbath have this concept of "oneg" as their major theme. One of them traditionally sung at the Friday night meal, "Mah Yedidut," has a refrain that begins "to indulge in delights . . ." One of the first delights mentioned in the first verse is kindling the Sabbath lights.

The reason that the Sabbath candles are considered a delight is simply because they provide light. According to our sages, light in the home was of critical importance. Not only did light provide practical assistance by preventing people from falling and suffering on the Sabbath, it also provided "shalom bayit," peace in the household.

Serenity and contentment could only be achieved by having lights lit in the house. This light and the peace that it brought were so important that Rabbi Joseph Karo, the author of the Shulchan Aruch (the most important code of Jewish law, completed in the 16th century in Safed, Israel), ruled that if one was very poor and only had enough money to purchase the bare necessities for Shabbat, candles were to take precedence over anything else.

This reason for the lighting of Shabbat candles should make it clear that it is an obligation for a household to have lights burning. Although women usually light the candles, if no women are present, men are obligated to light them.

The reason that, traditionally, two candles are lit is based on the text of the Ten Commandments. They appear twice in the Torah, first in Exodus when they were actually given, then in Deuteronomy when Moses reviews most of the Torah with the people before his death.

While these two accounts of the Ten Commandments are basically identical, there are some important differences. One is the commandment pertaining to Shabbat. In Exodus (20:8), we are commanded to "Remember [zachor] the Sabbath day to keep it holy." In Deuteronomy (5:12), we are told to "Guard [shamor] the Sabbath day to keep it holy."

The rabbis use these two different words to teach us about different categories of commandments that we must uphold on the Sabbath. We light two candles in remembrance of the two words—zachor and shamor—that signify two methods of sanctifying the Sabbath.

This does not mean, however, that one is not permitted to light more than two candles. Two is the minimum.

Some women light seven candles in accordance with the seven days of the week, and some light ten to signify the Ten Commandments. Another custom that some women have adopted is to light an additional candle (beyond the two) for each of their children. (Written by Rabbi Shlomo Levin. Copyright 2002 by *The Wisconsin Jewish Chronicle*. Reprinted by permission)

ABOUT THE PRAYER

The Sabbath is the first holiday named in the Torah, and in some ways it's more important than most of the other holidays, even though it occurs one a week and they only happen once each year. That's why in the festival version of the prayer, Shabbat is still mentioned first: even though it's a holiday, it's important to remember the Sabbath is a special time. Keeping the Sabbath holy was so important that in Biblical times, people could be put to death for ignoring Shabbat (although even in the Torah that didn't happen except in very rare cases). There's an old folk tradition that if all Jews keep the Sabbath for two weeks in a row, the messiah will come.

Shabbat is often translated as a *day of rest*, but that isn't exactly what the word means. Shabbat doesn't mean to rest, but to stop working. You may not need to rest on the Sabbath (and God didn't need to rest after creating the universe), but it's a time to stop working and thinking about the outside world so we can focus on the spiritual side of our lives.

LIGHTING THE CANDLES

נר של שבת

Barukh atah Adonay,
Blessed are You, oh God

eloheinu melekh ha olam,
our lord, king of all creation

ah sher keed shahnu bi meetzvotav,
whose commandments make us holy

vit zee vahnu, li had leek neir
and who commands us to light the candles

shel Shabat.
of sabbath

בָּרוּךְ אַתָּה יְיָ
אֱלֹהֵינוּ מֶלֶךְ הָעוֹלָם
אֲשֶׁר קִדְּשָׁנוּ בְּמִצְוֹתָיו
וְצִוָּנוּ לְהַדְלִיק נֵר
שֶׁל שַׁבָּת:

TRANSLATIONS (choose one)

Blessed are You, our lord and king, ruler of all creation, whose laws make us holy and by whose command we light the Sabbath candles.

Blessed are You, O lord our God, king of the universe, who sanctifies us by Thy commandments, and commands us to kindle the Sabbath lights.

Blessed are You, oh God, ruler of our people and of all creation, whose laws make us holy and who tells us to light the Sabbath candles.

LIGHTING THE FESTIVAL CANDLES

When shabbat falls on a holiday, use this version of the prayer instead.

Barukh atah Adonay,
Blessed are You, oh God

eloheinu melekh ha olam,
our lord, king of all creation

ah sher keed shahnu bi meetzvotav,
whose commandments make us holy

vit zee vahnu, li had leek neir
and who commands us to light the candles

shel Shabat vi yom tov.
of the sabbath and festivals

בָּרוּךְ אַתָּה יְיָ
אֱלֹהֵינוּ מֶלֶךְ הָעוֹלָם
אֲשֶׁר קִדְּשָׁנוּ בְּמִצְוֹתָיו
וְצִוָּנוּ לְהַדְלִיק נֵר
שֶׁל שַׁבָּת וְיוֹם טוֹב:

TRANSLATIONS (choose one)

Blessed are You, our lord and king, ruler of all creation, whose laws make us holy and by whose command we light the Sabbath and holiday candles.

Blessed are You, O lord our God, king of the universe, who sanctifies us by Thy commandments, and commands us to kindle the Sabbath and festival lights.

Blessed are You, oh God, ruler of our people and of all creation, whose laws make us holy and who tells us to light candles on the Sabbath and on holy days.

ABOUT THE SONGS

There is a strong tradition of singing as a community in Judaism. Because they are meant to be sung together in a group, many of the songs are simple and easily learned, even for people who don't know much Hebrew. While some songs are deeply poetic, many of the songs we sing before shabbat are just short expressions of joy that can be sung to many tunes (and in rounds). They are filled with puns and nonsense phrases, more concerned with sound than meaning. The idea of the songs is to relax us and put us in the mood for the Sabbath, part of the process of letting go of the past week's care and worries.

The word *shalom* is used as a greeting like *hello* or *goodbye*, but its literal meaning is *peace*. The sabbath is a time of peace and calm, a time to take a break from the stress of our everyday lives. Shabbat is a time to reconnect with our families and what's important in our lives, a time to be focused and centered. It's not just a time of physical relaxation, but a rest for all of our senses (which is why the short *Havdala* ceremony at the end of the Sabbath is focused on reawakening our senses for the week to come).

The phrase *bim bom* appears as a refrain in many Yiddish-language songs, and doesn't mean anything in particular. Hasidic songs are filled with B, D, and Y sounds (like *bim bom, ya ba bom, di dom,* and *yadi yadi*) while Lubavitch songs more often use M, N, and Y sounds (like *na na na, ni nam, ma ma m*a, or *oy oy*).

The phrase *hi nei ma to vu* comes from the first verse of Psalm 133:

Behold how good and pleasant it is for brethren to dwell together in unity. (JPS 1917)

Psalm 96 (*Oh sing unto the Lord a new song; sing unto the Lord all the earth*) has been used as part of the pre-Shabbat singing since at least the sixteenth century. *Yees mihkhu hashamayim* comes from verse 11 of the psalm.

Yees mihkhu bimalkhutkha is a traditional adaptation from Isaiah:

If thou turn away thy foot because of the sabbath, from pursuing thy business on My holy day, and call the sabbath a delight . . . then shalt thou delight thyself in the Lord. (58:13-14, JPS 1917)

THE SABBATH HOUSE

This is a modern adaptation from Psalm 84. Metaphorically we are on the doorstep of God's house as we light candles and sing songs for shabbat, preparing ourselves emotionally to enter a holy place.

Your house is beautiful, oh, Lord of our people.
My soul longs for the corridors of your house;
My heart and body sing with joy to You.

> The sparrow finds a home; the swallow builds a
> nest to lay her eggs.
> Their homes are altars to You: our Lord, our
> King, our God.

Happy are those who live in Your house: They sing
with joy to be near You.
Happy are those who draw their strength from love of
You,
Whose hearts sing to you while they walk the paths
that lead to Your house.

> They pass through the valley where Your springs
> well up,
> Where the spring rains clothe the land with Your
> blessings.
> They pass through beauty as they draw close to
> your house.

Lord of our people, please hear my prayer
As You heard Jacob's prayers.
Lord, our shield, see me as I sing to You.

> A day in Your house is more precious to me
> than a thousand days outside it.
> I would rather stand on the doorstep of Your
> house
> Than live in a palace that stands outside your
> paths.

Our God, You are a sun and a shield;
Our Lord, You give grace and glory and all good
things
To those who walk willingly on the path that You
created.
Lord of our people: Blessed are those who trust in
You.

WELCOMING SHABBAT

קַבָּלַת שַׁבָּת

מַה יָּפֶה הַיּוֹם. שַׁבָּת שָׁלוֹם.

בִּם בַּם. שַׁבָּת שָׁלוֹם.

הִנֵּה מַה טּוֹב וּמַה נָּעִים
שֶׁבֶת אַחִים גַּם יָחַד:

הָבָה נָשִׁירָה שִׁיר הַלְלוּיָהּ.

פִּתְחוּ־לִי שַׁעֲרֵי־צֶדֶק
אָבֹא בָם אוֹדֶה יָהּ.

וְטַהֵר לִבֵּנוּ לְעָבְדְּךָ בֶּאֱמֶת.

יִשְׂמְחוּ הַשָּׁמַיִם וְתָגֵל הָאָרֶץ
יִרְעַם הַיָּם וּמְלֹאוֹ.

יִשְׂמְחוּ בְמַלְכוּתְךָ שׁוֹמְרֵי שַׁבָּת
וְקוֹרְאֵי עֹנֶג. עַם מְקַדְּשֵׁי שְׁבִיעִי
כֻּלָּם יִשְׂבְּעוּ וְיִתְעַנְּגוּ מִטּוּבֶךָ.
וְהַשְּׁבִיעִי רָצִיתָ בּוֹ וְקִדַּשְׁתּוֹ.
חֶמְדַּת יָמִים אוֹתוֹ קָרָאתָ זֵכֶר
לְמַעֲשֵׂה בְרֵאשִׁית.

Ma ya fe ha yom. Shabat shalom.
What a pretty day. Have a peaceful shabbat.

Beem bom. Shabat shalom.
Bim bom. Sabbath greetings.

Hee nei ma to vu ma na yeem.
Look how very good and very pleasant it is
Shevet ah kheem gom yah khad.
to relax as a community together

Hava nasheera sheer ha lih lu ya.
We sing a song of praise.

Peet khu lee sha ah rei tze dek.
Open for me the gates of wisdom and holiness;
Ah vo vam oh deh ya.
I will pass through them, giving thanks to the Lord.

Vihta heir leebeinu lih av di kha be ehmet.
Purify our hearts so we may serve You with certainty.

Yees mihkhu hashamayim vihtageil haaretz
Let the heavens be glad. Let the earth rejoice.
yir am ha yam umihloh oh.
Let the sea and all within it roar.

Yees mihkhu bimalkhutkha shomrei Shabat
Welcome to your dominion those who welcome the Sabbath
vikorei oneg. Am mikadishei shivee yee
and who take joy in it. May those who keep holy the seventh day
culam yeesbi u viyeet angu mee tuvekha.
have goodness and satisfaction in their lives.
Vihashvee yee ratzeeta bo vikeedashto.
For You have blessed the seventh day and made it holy,
Khemdat yameem ohto ka ra ta zeikher
calling it the most important day, in remembrance
li ma a sei vireisheet.
of all that You created.

ABOUT THE PRAYER

We traditionally open our Friday night service with this hymn. The song is comparatively new; it was written in the seventeenth century by members of the Kabbalic community (possibly in Safed, one of four holy cities in Israel, along with Jerusalem, Hebron, and Tiberias. Safed is in the mountains of Galilee in northern Israel, and you can still visit it today).

Originally, the hymn was sung after returning from Friday evening services, just before sitting down for sabbath dinner.

The song is based on a story in the Talmud (*Shabbat* 119b), in which a person returning from services is accompanied by two angels, one good and one evil. When the person gets home if the house is clean, a light is on, dinner is ready, and the beds are made, the good angel says, "May it be God's will that things will be the same way next sabbath," and the evil angel has no choice but to say, "Amen." But if the person gets home and the house is dark and messy and nothing is ready, then the evil angel says, "May it be God's will that things will be the same way next sabbath," and this time the good angel has no choice but to say, "Amen."

If two angels are guiding you home and keeping you safe, it's only polite to thank them and bless them, and ask for their blessing in return, which is what the song does: The first verse is a blessing on the angels that guide us, the second welcomes them into our home for the sabbath, the third asks for God's blessing through them, and the fourth wishes them peace on their journey to wherever God sends them next.

In the first verse, the guardians are called "guiding angels," but after that, the song refers to them as "angels of peace." Some rabbis say that the first verse refers to *all* angels, blessing all of the many guardians God sends to look after us, while the rest of the verses refer only to the two angels in the Talmudic story.

The song emphasizes the holiness of the sabbath and the importance of preparing both our homes and our spirits for this special time of grounding and reconnecting with what's holy in the world around us, and leaving our everyday concerns behind. In other words, a household that's ready for the sabbath is so holy that even an angel is blessed by entering it.

TRANSLATION

Peace be on you, guiding angels,
Messengers of the holiest one,
The king of kings: Blessed is He.

Come in peace, angels of peace,
Messengers of the holiest one,
The king of kings: Blessed is He.

Bless me with God's peace, angels of peace,
Messengers of the holiest one,
The king of kings: Blessed is He.

Leave in peace, angels of peace,
Messengers of the holiest one,
The king of kings: Blessed is He.

ALTERNATE VERSION

The Sephardic version of the hymn adds another verse before the last stanza:

Shiv ti khem li shalom. Malikhei ha shalom.
Malikhei elyon
Mi melekh malikhei hamlakheem.
Ha kadosh barukh hoo:

This verse asks the angels to stay in peace for a while before leaving: the sabbath is a happy, relaxing time, why rush to leave? Sit and enjoy yourself first.

SHALOM ALEIKHEM

שלום עליכם

Shalom aleikhem. Malakhei ha shareit.
Peace be on you, guiding angels,
Malakhei elyon.
Messengers of the holiest one,
Mee melekh malakhei hamlakheem.
The king of kings,
Ha kadosh barukh hoo.
Blessed is He.

שָׁלוֹם עֲלֵיכֶם. מַלְאֲכֵי הַשָּׁרֵת.

מַלְאֲכֵי עֶלְיוֹן.

מִמֶּלֶךְ מַלְכֵי הַמְּלָכִים.

הַקָּדוֹשׁ בָּרוּךְ הוּא:

Bo akhem li shalom. Malakhei ha shalom.
Come in peace, angels of peace,
Malakhei elyon.
Messengers of the holiest one,
Mee melekh malakhei hamlakheem.
The king of kings,
Ha kadosh barukh hoo.
Blessed is He.

בּוֹאֲכֶם לְשָׁלוֹם. מַלְאֲכֵי הַשָּׁלוֹם.

מַלְאֲכֵי עֶלְיוֹן.

מִמֶּלֶךְ מַלְכֵי הַמְּלָכִים.

הַקָּדוֹשׁ בָּרוּךְ הוּא:

Barkhuni li shalom. Malakhei ha shalom.
Bless me with God's peace, angels of peace,
Malakhei elyon.
Messengers of the holiest one,
Mee melekh malakhei hamlakheem.
The king of kings,
Ha kadosh barukh hoo.
Blessed is He.

בָּרְכוּנִי לְשָׁלוֹם. מַלְאֲכֵי הַשָּׁלוֹם.

מַלְאֲכֵי עֶלְיוֹן.

מִמֶּלֶךְ מַלְכֵי הַמְּלָכִים.

הַקָּדוֹשׁ בָּרוּךְ הוּא:

Tzay ti khem li shalom. Malakhei ha shalom.
Leave in peace, angels of peace,
Malakhei elyon.
Messengers of the holiest one,
Mee melekh malakhei hamlakheem.
The king of kings,
Ha kadosh barukh hoo.
Blessed is He.

צֵאתְכֶם לְשָׁלוֹם. מַלְאֲכֵי הַשָּׁלוֹם.

מַלְאֲכֵי עֶלְיוֹן.

מִמֶּלֶךְ מַלְכֵי הַמְּלָכִים.

הַקָּדוֹשׁ בָּרוּךְ הוּא:

ABOUT THE PRAYER

Ma Tovu is the traditional prayer said on entering the synagogue for services. (We usually sing the first verse in Hebrew, then read the whole prayer in English.) It isn't actually a part of the formal service; like the songs after lighting the candles, it's designed to get us in the proper frame of mind to welcome the sabbath.

Instead of being a single prayer, the Ma Tovu is a collection of verses on related themes, taken from different parts of the Torah, that come together into a song that expresses the mix of joy and awe that we fell on coming into God's house, as we do symbolically when we enter the sanctuary of the synagogue to pray. The first sentence of the prayer is from Numbers 24:5, while the others are all taken from Psalms (5:8, 26:8, a paraphrase of 95:6, and 69:14).

The passage in Numbers is from the story of Balaam, who was ordered to curse the people of israel, but instead blessed them, saying:

> How goodly are thy tents, O Jacob, thy dwellings, oh Israel!
> As valleys stretched out, as gardens by the riverside, as aloes planted of the Lord, as cedars beside the waters;
> Water shall flow from his branches, and his seed shall be in many water; and his king shall be higher than Agag, and his kingdom shall be exalted.
> God who brought him forth out of Egypt is for him like the lofty horns of the wild ox; he shall eat up the nations that are his adversaries, and shall break their bones in pieces, and pierce them through with his arrows.
> He couched, he lay down as a lion, and as a lioness; who shall rouse him up? Blessed be every one that blesseth thee, and cursed be every one that curseth thee. (JPS 1917)

Since the prayer is a compilation of verses rather than a complete paragraph, it can be translated in many ways, and interpreted to mean more than on thing. The translation here emphasizes the joy and overwhelming emotions we feel when we enter God's house (whether that entrance is physical, spiritual, or metaphorical). Other translations may emphasize our sense of worship, or even fear of God. Two other poetic translations are included here as alternate readings.

TRANSLATION

May the homes of your people be sound, oh Jacob;
May the homes of your people be well, oh Israel.

Your kindness welcomes me into Your house, oh God,
and there I bow down in awe and love of You.

I love the moments I spend in Your house,
the moments I **am** nearer to Your glory.

I bow down and worship You in Your house,
You who made all of us.

Please accept my prayer, Oh merciful God,
and answer me with knowledge and with wisdom.

MA TOVU

מַה־טֹבוּ

Ma tovu oh ha leykha ya ah kov
Good are your tents, Jacob

מַה־טֹּבוּ אֹהָלֶיךָ יַעֲקֹב.

meesh ki no tekha yis ra eil.
your hourses, Israel.

מִשְׁכְּנֹתֶיךָ יִשְׂרָאֵל:

Va nee bi rov khasdikha, ahvo bei te kha.
and I with your great loving kindness shall enter your house

וַאֲנִי בְּרֹב חַסְדְּךָ. אָבֹא בֵיתֶךָ.

eshta khaveh el hei khol
I shall prostrate myself toward Your temple

אֶשְׁתַּחֲוֶה אֶל־הֵיכַל

kad shi kha bi yee ra tehkha
that is holy in the fear of You.

קָדְשְׁךָ בְּיִרְאָתֶךָ:

Adonay ah havtee mi ohn bei tekha,
God, I love the dwelling of Your house

יְיָ אָהַבְתִּי מְעוֹן בֵּיתֶךָ.

u mikom meeshkan ki voh dekha
and the place of the residence of Your glory.

וּמְקוֹם מִשְׁכַּן כְּבוֹדֶךָ:

va anee esh ta kha vee vi ekhra ah
Come, let us prostrate ourselves and bow;

וַאֲנִי אֶשְׁתַּחֲוֶה וְאֶכְרָעָה.

ev rikha leef nei Adonay eeh shee.
let us kneel before You, our Maker.

אֶבְרְכָה לִפְנֵי־יְיָ עֹשִׂי:

va ahnee ti fee la tee likha Adonai,
But, as for me, may my prayer to You

וַאֲנִי תְפִלָּתִי לְךָ יְיָ.

eit ra tzon eh lo heem,
be in an acceptable time

עֵת רָצוֹן אֱלֹהִים.

bi rov khas de kha ah nei nee
with Your abundant kindness

בְּרָב־חַסְדֶּךָ עֲנֵנִי

beh eh met yees eh kha
answer me with the truth of Your salvation.

בֶּאֱמֶת יִשְׁעֶךָ:

ABOUT THE PRAYER

The ninety-fifth Psalm starts out as a song of joy and praise to God, and ends up as a dark warning of what happens when the people of Israel anger God. Most services focus on the opening verses, with their spontaneous outpouring of joy at God's love and creation. Those opening verses are reproduced in the Hebrew here.

There are several tunes, all of which tend to be upbeat, not surprisingly.

There are six psalms often read before the beginning of the service, Psalms 95-99 and Psalm 29. All of them emphasize God's power over the universe. In addition to Psalm 95, the other five are reproduced in English here and on the next two pages.

PSALM 95

O come, let us sing unto the Lord; let us shout for joy to the Rock of our salvation.
Let us come before His presence with thanksgiving, let us shout for joy unto Him with psalms.
For the Lord is a great God, and a great King above all gods;
In whose hand are the depths of the earth; the heights of the mountains are His also.
The sea is His, and He made it; and His hands formed the dry land.
O come, let us bow down and bend the knee; let us kneel before the Lord our Maker;
For He is our God, and we are the people of His pasture, and the flock of His hand. To-day, if ye would but hearken to His voice!
"Harden not your heart, as at Meribah, as in the day of Massah in the wilderness;
When your fathers tried Me, proved Me, even though they saw My work.
For forty years was I wearied with that generation, and said: It is a people that do err in their heart, and they have not known My ways;
Wherefore I swore in My wrath, that they should not enter into My rest." (JPS 1917)

PSALM 96

We sing unto You a new song; sing unto You, all the earth.

We sing unto You, bless Your name; proclaim Your salvation from day to day.

We declare Your glory among the nations, Your marvelous works among all the peoples.

For great are You, and highly to be praised; You are to be feared above all gods.

For all the idols of other peoples have produced nothing; but You made the heavens.

Honor and majesty are before You; strength and beauty are in Your sanctuary.

We ascribe unto You, with all of our hearts, we ascribe unto You glory and strength.

We ascribe You the glory due unto Your name; we bring offerings, and come into Your courts.

Worship God in the beauty of holiness; tremble before Him, all the earth.

Say among the nations: God is the king of all. The world You established cannot be moved;

You will judge all peoples with equity.

Let the heavens be glad, and let the earth rejoice; let the sea roar, and celebrate with its noise;

Let the fields exult; and all that is therein; then shall all the trees of the wood sing for joy;

Before You, for You have come to judge the earth;

You will judge the world with righteousness, and the peoples in His faithfulness. (adapted from JPS 1917)

LI KHU NI RANI NA

לְכוּ נְרַנְּנָה

לְכוּ נְרַנְּנָה לַיְיָ

Li khu ni rani na la Adonay

Come, let us sing happily to You

נָרִיעָה לְצוּר יִשְׁעֵנוּ:

na ree ah litzor yee seinu.

let us shout out to the rock of our redemption.

נְקַדְּמָה פָנָיו בְּתוֹדָה

Ni kadma fa nayv bi todah

Let us greet You with thanks

בִּזְמִרוֹת נָרִיעַ לוֹ:

beez meerot na ree ah lo.

with praising songs let us cry out to You.

כִּי אֵל גָּדוֹל יְיָ

Kee eil gadol Adonay

A great God are You

וּמֶלֶךְ גָּדוֹל עַל־כָּל־אֱלֹהִים:

ume melekh gadol al col eloheem.

and a king great above all other gods.

אֲשֶׁר בְּיָדוֹ מֶחְקְרֵי־אָרֶץ

Asher bi yado mekhkirei aretz

for in Your powerr are the hidden mysteries of the land

וְתוֹעֲפוֹת הָרִים לוֹ:

vi to afot hareem lo.

and the tops of the mountains are Yours.

אֲשֶׁר־לוֹ הַיָּם וְהוּא עָשָׂהוּ

Asher lo hayam vi hu asahu

For Yours is the sea and You perfected it

וְיַבֶּשֶׁת יָדָיו יָצָרוּ:

vi yabeshet yadayv yatzaru.

and the dry land Your hands fashioned.

בֹּאוּ נִשְׁתַּחֲוֶה וְנִכְרָעָה

Bo u neeshtakha veh vi neekhra a

Come, let us prostrate ourselves and bow

נִבְרְכָה לִפְנֵי־יְיָ עֹשֵׂנוּ:

neevrikha leefnei Adonay oseinu.

Let us kneel before You our maker.

כִּי הוּא אֱלֹהֵינוּ

Kee hu eloheinu

For You are our God

וַאֲנַחְנוּ עַם מַרְעִיתוֹ וְצֹאן יָדוֹ:

vi anakhnu am mareetu vi tzon yado.

and we the flock you tend and the sheep you watch.

PSALM 97

You rule over us; let all the earth rejoice; let the
multitude of isles be glad.

Clouds and darkness are round about You;
righteousness and justice are the foundation
of Your throne.

A fire blazes the way before You, and burns
Your adversaries with heavenly power.

Your lightnings lights up the world; the earth
sees, and trembles.

The mountains melt like wax at Your presence,
at the presence of the God of the whole
earth.

The heavens declare Your righteousness, and all
the peoples see Your glory.

Ashamed are those who serve graven images,
who boost themselves with things made of
nothing; all other gods bow down to bow
down to You.

Zion heard and was glad, and the daughters of
Judah rejoiced because of Your judgments.

For You art most high above all the earth; You
are exalted far above all gods.

Know that those of us who love You, hate evil;
You preserv the souls of Your saints; You
deliver them out of the hands of the wicked.

Light is sown for the righteous, and gladness for
the upright in heart.

We are glad in You, if we are righteous; and
we give thanks to Your holy name. (adapted
from JPS 1917)

PSALM 98

We sing unto You a new song; for You have
done marvelous things;

Your right hand, and Your holy arm, have made
salvation for us.

You have shown us Your salvation; Your righteousness You have revealed in the sight of
the world.

You have shown mercy and faithfulness toward
the house of Israel; all the ends of the earth
have seen the salvation of our God.

Shout unto You, all the earth; break forth and
sing for joy, sing Your praises. We sing
praises unto You with the harp and the voice
of melody.

With trumpets and horns we proclaim our joy
before You, our King.

Let the sea roar, and celebrate with its noise, to
all the world, and they that dwell therein;

Let the waters clap their hands; let the mountains sing for joy together before You, for You
are come to judge the earth;

You will judge the world with righteousness,
and all its peoples with equity. (adapted from
JPS 1917)

PSALM 99

You rule over us; let the peoples tremble; You
are enthroned upon Your angels; let the earth
quake.

You are great in Zion; and You are high above
all the peoples.

Let them praise Your name as great and overpowering; Holy are You.

You use Your strength as a king who loves justice. You treat all with equity, You execute justice and expect righteousness from us.

We exalt You, our God, and prostrate ourselves
at Your footstool; Holy are You.

Moses and Aaron were among Your priests,
and Samuel among those who called upon
Your name, and You answered them.

You spoke unto them in the pillar of cloud; they
kept Your testimonies, and the laws that You
gave them.

You answered them and forgave them, though
You took vengeance against their misdeeds.

We exalt You, our God, and worship at Your
holy hill; for You, our God, are holy. (adapted
from JPS 1917)

PSALM 29

We ascribe unto You, O children of might,
ascribe unto You glory and strength.

We ascribe unto You the glory due to Your
name; we worship You in the beauty of holiness.

Your voice is upon the waters; the God of glory
thunders upon many waters.

Your voice is powerful; Your voice is full of
majesty.

Your voice shatters the cedars; You break in
pieces the cedars of Lebanon. You make
them skip like a calf; Lebanon and Syrian like
a young wild ox.

Your voice lights the darkness with flames of
fire. Your voice shakes the wilderness; You
shake the wilderness of Kadesh.

Your voice makes the hinds to calve, and strips
the forests bare; and in Your temple all say:
Glory.

You sit enthroned at the flood; You sit as King
forever.

You will give strength unto Your people; You will
bless Your people with peace. (adapted from
JPS 1917)

THE SABBATH QUEEN

Traditionally, the congregation rises before the last verse of the song and faces the door, as if welcoming the arrival of the Sabbath Queen. Everyone bows at the beginning of the last line, and straighten before the final chorus.

The idea of using the image of a queen as a metaphor for the Sabbath is an old one. This particular song, written in the sixteenth century by Rabbi Shlomo Ha Levee Alkabetz, was the most popular and is the only one that remains widely known. Like many traditional Hebrew songs and prayers, it's filled with clever wordplay, playfulness, and hidden meanings that only become available on deeper study. For instance, the first letter of the first eight stanzas form an acrostic of the author's name.

The arrival of the Sabbath signifies a time for leaving the tumult of everyday life to live at ease for a day, as one would in a palace. We put an end to work or everyday concerns, the way we put aside our everyday lives in the presence of royalty. The metaphor is furrther extended by taking it from an individual celebrating laying down his or her cares at the end of the week with the laying down of cares that will come to the whole world with the coming of the Messiah.

The song is also distinct for describing an aspect of God's presence in feminine rather than masculine terms. While translations of the Torah and Talmud tend to be more gendered than the original because of the dearth of non-gendered pronouns in English, it's much more common to find prayers that describe God's relationship with the Jewish people as being like one's relationship with a king or a lord or a father than like one's relationship with a a queen or mother. But there's nothing gendered about our relationship with God; the gender is in the terms and metaphors we use to attempt to understand the Torah.

The translation on this page is true to the metaphor, rather than a literal translation. Subtle references to the lineage of the Messiah that would be lost on audiences not steeped in Hebrew history and genealogy have been made clearer while retaining the central metaphor.

TRANSLATION

Come, loved one, to greet the bride.
We welcome the Sabbath Queen's return.

> Protect and remember the words that were said.
> That we heard because we listened to You.
> You are one and your name is first
> In fame, in glory, and in our prayers.

Let us go then, to welcome the Sabbath Queen,
For she is the source of blessings.
From ancient times, we have honored her arrival.
When our work is done, she is first in our thoughts.

> See the Palace of the King, the city of royalty.
> Rise up and depart from the daily tumult!
> For too long you have lived in a valley of tears;
> In the palace you will find compassion.

Shake the dust from your clothes and rise up
Put on your festival clothes, My people
Prepare for the day when the Messiah comes
to touch your soul and redeem it in My name.

> Wake up, wake up!
> For morning is coming, and with it the light.
> Wake up, wake up, and sing—
> For My glory has been revealed to you.

Do not feel ashamed or embarrassed.
Cast off your sadness when you enter My house.
Inside there is shelter, and freedom from suffering.
My city will soon be rebuilt on its hilltop.

> Those who trampled on you will be trampled.
> Those who feasted on you will be outcast.
> Rejoice in the presence of my Sabbath Queen
> Like a groom rejoices before his bride.

In all directions will My people grow
And everywhere you shall sing My praises.
With the coming of My Messiah
All shall be glad and filled with laughter.

> My queen comes in peace with her Sabbath crown.
> She brings happiness and celebration with her
> to all who are faithful, to My treasured people—
> enter, bride, enter bride.

LI KHA DO DEE   לְכָה דוֹדִי

CHORUS (sing this twice, then repeat after each verse)

Li kha do dee lee krat ka la *Come loved one to greet the bride*	לְכָה דוֹדִי לִקְרַאת כַּלָּה.
pi nei shabat ni kabla. *the presence of the Sabbath we welcome.*	פְּנֵי שַׁבָּת נְקַבְּלָה:

Shamor vi zakhor bi deebor ekhad *Protect and remember what was said once*	שָׁמוֹר וְזָכוֹר בְּדִבּוּר אֶחָד.
hee shmeeyanu eil hamiyukhad *that we heard because of God the one and only*	הִשְׁמִיעָנוּ אֵל הַמְיֻחָד.
Adonai ekhad ushimo ekhad *God is one and God's name is one*	יְיָ אֶחָד וּשְׁמוֹ אֶחָד.
li sheim ul teeferet vi lee ti hee la. *in fame, and in magnificence, and in praise.*	לְשֵׁם וּלְתִפְאֶרֶת וְלִתְהִלָּה:

(chorus)

Lee krat shabat li khu vi neilkha *To welcome the Sabbath, come let us go*	לִקְרַאת שַׁבָּת לְכוּ וְנֵלְכָה.
keehee mi kor ha bi rakha *for it is the source of blessings*	כִּי הִיא מְקוֹר הַבְּרָכָה.
mei rosh mee kedem ni su kha *from the beginning, from ancient times, she was honored*	מֵרֹאשׁ מִקֶּדֶם נְסוּכָה.
sof ma aseh bi makha shava ti hee la. *last in actions but foremost in thoughts.*	סוֹף מַעֲשֶׂה בְּמַחֲשָׁבָה תְּחִלָּה:

(chorus)

Meekdosh melekh eer mi lukha *Palace of the King, city of royalty*	מִקְדַּשׁ מֶלֶךְ עִיר מְלוּכָה.
kumee tzi ee mee tokh ha ha fei kha *rise up and depart from amid the tumult*	קוּמִי צְאִי מִתּוֹךְ הַהֲפֵכָה.
rav lakh shevet bi eimek habakha *for too long you have lived in the valley of crying*	רַב לָךְ שֶׁבֶת בְּעֵמֶק הַבָּכָא.
vihoo yakhamol alayeekh khemla. *God will with understanding show you compassion.*	וְהוּא יַחֲמֹל עָלַיִךְ חֶמְלָה:

(chorus)

Heetna aree mei afar kumee *Shake off the dust and rise up*	הִתְנַעֲרִי מֵעָפָר קוּמִי.
leevshee beegdei teef artekh amee *Put on you clothes that are fancy, my people*	לִבְשִׁי בִּגְדֵי תִפְאַרְתֵּךְ עַמִּי.
alyad ben yeeshahy beit halakhmee *through tthe son of Jesse of Bethlehem*	עַל־יַד בֶּן יִשַׁי בֵּית הַלַּחְמִי.
karva el nafshee ga la. *move close to my soul and redeem it*	קָרְבָה אֶל נַפְשִׁי גְאָלָהּ:

PRAYER TO BE SAID WHEN GOING ON A JOURNEY

Metaphorically, at least, each Sabbath marks the end of one journey and the beginning of another. This modern adaptation from DPB 1914 speaks as much to spiritual journeys as to literal ones.

> May it be Your will, oh Lord our God and God of our parents, to conduct us in peace, to direct our steps in peace, to uphold us in peace, and to lead us in life, joy, and peace to the haven where we desire to go. Please deliver us from enemy, ambush, and hurt along the way, and from all the sorrows that visit and trouble this world.

> Send a blessing upon the work of our hands. Let us obtain grace, kindness, love, and mercy in Your eyes and in the eyes of others who who look upon us.

> Hear the voice of our supplications; for You are a God who listens and considers our prayers and supplications. Blessed are You, oh Lord, who listens to our prayers.

> And Jacob went on his way, and the angels of God met him. And when Jacob saw them, he said, This is the camp of God: and he called the name of that place Mahanaim, a double camp. Behold, I send an angel before you, to keep you safely along the path, and to bring you into the place which I have prepared.

> The Lord bless you and keep you. May the Lord make his face to shine upon you. May the Lord turn his face unto you, and give you peace. Let the pleasantness of the Lord our God be upon you, and may the work of your hands be blessed.

> You are my shelter. You will preserve me from trouble. You will surround me and guard me with songs of deliverance. Trust in the Lord forever, for our Lord is an everlasting rock. The Lord of hosts is with us: the God of our parents is our stronghold. Oh Lord of hosts, happy is the one who trusts in You. Save us and protect us, oh Lord. May You answer us on the day when we call.

I LIFT MY EYES

This is a modern adaptation from Psalm 121. The psalm is sometimes said as a part of the afternoon prayers, and as a part of the prayer said before going on a journey.

> I lift my eyes unto the hills and ask,
> Where will my help come from?

> My help is from You, oh Lord,
> You made the heaven and the earth.
> My feet will not slip while You watch over them.

> The Lord that guards me does not slumber.
> The guardian of Israel neither sleeps nor slumbers.
> You are my guardian, oh Lord.

> You are the shade that protects me.
> The sun will not harm me by day
> Nor the moon by night,
> While You watch over me.

> The Lord guards me from all evil.
> You are the guardian of my soul, oh Lord.

> You guard me when I go out
> and when I come in,
> You guard me from this day forward
> and for evermore.

Hee to ri ree hee to ri ree

Wake up, wake up

kee va oreikh kumee uree

for coming is the light, rise up and shine

uree uree sheer da bei ree

wake up, wake up, a song belt out

ki vod Adonai alayeekh neegla.

the glory of God to you has been revealed.

(chorus)

הִתְעוֹרְרִי הִתְעוֹרְרִי.

כִּי בָא אוֹרֵךְ קוּמִי אוֹרִי.

עוּרִי עוּרִי שִׁיר דַבֵּרִי.

כְּבוֹד יְיָ עָלַיִךְ נִגְלָה:

Lo tei vi shee vi lo teekal mee

Do not feel ashamed, do not feel embarrassed

ma teeshto khakhee uma te he mee

why are you melancholy? why are you sad?

bekh ye khesu anee yei amee

inside you will find shelter, those who suffer among My people

vi neev ni ta eer al teela.

because rebuilt will the city be on its hilltop.

(chorus)

לֹא תֵבְשִׁי וְלֹא תִכָּלְמִי.

מַה תִּשְׁתּוֹחֲחִי וּמַה תֶּהֱמִי.

בָּךְ יֶחֱסוּ עֲנִיֵּי עַמִּי.

וְנִבְנְתָה עִיר עַל תִּלָּהּ:

vi ha yu leemsheesa shosa yeekh

They will be trampled, those who trampled you

vi rakha ku kol mi va la yeekh

and outcast will be all who feasted on you

ya sees alayeekh elo ha yeekh

rejoice for in you will your God

keemsos khatan al kala.

like the rejoicing of a groom over his bride.

(chorus)

וְהָיוּ לִמְשִׁסָּה שֹׁאסָיִךְ.

וְרָחֲקוּ כָּל־מְבַלְּעָיִךְ.

יָשִׂישׂ עָלַיִךְ אֱלֹהָיִךְ.

כִּמְשׂוֹשׂ חָתָן עַל כַּלָּה:

Ya meen usma ol teef ra tzee

To the right and to the left you shall expand greatly.

vi et Adonai ta aree tzee

and of God you shall sing the praises

al yad eesh ben pa ree tzee

through the man descended from Peretz

vi nees mikha vi na geela.

then we shall be glad and filled with laughter.

(chorus)

יָמִין וּשְׂמֹאל תִּפְרֹצִי.

וְאֶת יְיָ תַּעֲרִיצִי.

עַל יַד אִישׁ בֶּן פַּרְצִי.

וְנִשְׂמְחָה וְנָגִילָה:

Bo ee vishalom ateret ba ila

Enter in peace with the crown of her husband

gam bi seemkha uvtza hala

even in happiness and celebration

tokh emunei am si gula

among the faithful or our people most treasured

bo ee ca la bo ee ca la.

enter, bride, enter bride.

בּוֹאִי בְשָׁלוֹם עֲטֶרֶת בַּעְלָהּ.

גַּם בְּשִׂמְחָה וּבְצָהֳלָה.

תּוֹךְ אֱמוּנֵי עַם סְגֻלָּה.

בּוֹאִי כַלָּה בּוֹאִי כַלָּה:

ABOUT THE PRAYER

The ninety-third Psalm is the last prayer of the pre-Sabbath service (*Kabalat Shabat*). After the Kaddish, the congregation moves on to the *Maariv* (Shabat service). There is no actual pause between the "getting in the right frame of mind for the Sabbath" part of the service and the "giving thanks to God for the Sabbath" part of the service.

TRANSLATION

You rule over us; You are clothed in power and majesty. You wrap Yourself with power and strength like a mantle.

You have made the world like the strongest castle. It cannot be moved.

Your throne is ancient and eternal; Your kingdom will last forever.

The floods lift up to celebrate You, the floods lift up their voice; the floods lift up their roaring.

Above the voices of the surging waters, louder than the mighty breakers of the sea, Your presence is overpowering.

Your commandments are like prophecies, and holiness will come we who follow them. Holiness is forever in Your house. (adapted from JPS 1917)

ALTERNATE VERSIONS

The Lord reigneth; He is clothed in majesty;
the Lord is clothed, He hath girded Himself with strength;

Yea, the world is established, that it cannot be moved.

Thy throne is established of old;
Thou art from everlasting.

The floods have lifted up, O Lord,
the floods have lifted up their voice; the floods lift up their roaring.

Above the voices of many waters,
the mighty breakers of the sea,
the Lord on high is mighty.

Thy testimonies are very sure,
holiness becometh Thy house, O Lord, for evermore. (JPS 1917)

PSALM 93

יְיָ מֶלֶךְ גֵּאוּת

Adonay malakh gei ut la veish
God rules, and is dressed in power

la veish Adonay oz heet azar
dressed is God with dtrength

af teekon teiveil bal teemot.
the world is established, it cannot be moved

Nakhon kees akha ma az
established is Your throne of eternity

mei olam atah.
of everything are You

Nasu ni harot Adonay
the waters have lifted, O God

nasu ni harot kolam
the waters have lifted their voice

yee su ni harot dakh yam.
the floods lift up their roaring

Mee kolot ma yeem ra beem
above the voices of waters many

adee reem meesh bi ray yam
the mighty breakers of the sea

adeer ba marom Adonai.
on high is mighty our God

Eido teiykha ne emnu mi od
Your testimonies are very sure

li vei tikha na avah kodesh
to your house belongs holiness

Adonai li orekh ya meem.
God until the end of days.

יְיָ מָלַךְ גֵּאוּת לָבֵשׁ

לָבֵשׁ יְיָ עֹז הִתְאַזָּר

אַף־תִּכּוֹן תֵּבֵל בַּל־תִּמּוֹט:

נָכוֹן כִּסְאֲךָ מֵאָז

מֵעוֹלָם אָתָּה:

נָשְׂאוּ נְהָרוֹת יְיָ

נָשְׂאוּ נְהָרוֹת קוֹלָם

יִשְׂאוּ נְהָרוֹת דָּכְיָם:

מִקֹּלוֹת מַיִם רַבִּים

אַדִּירִים מִשְׁבְּרֵי־יָם

אַדִּיר בַּמָּרוֹם יְיָ:

עֵדֹתֶיךָ נֶאֶמְנוּ מְאֹד

לְבֵיתְךָ נַאֲוָה־קֹדֶשׁ

יְיָ לְאֹרֶךְ יָמִים:

ABOUT THE PRAYER

The *Kaddish* is one of the best known prayers in Judaism, and one of the most important. Although it is the prayer for the dead and for those in mourning, death is never mnentioned in the *Kaddish*. Instead, it is a celebration of God's relationship with us, and of the spiritual and physical renewal that comes from our connection with God. Ultimately, the purpose of the *Kaddish* is not to pray for peace for the dead, who are already at peace, but to comfort those who mourn for them, and remind them of the peace that comes from God's blessings.

Traditionally, *Kaddish* can only be said when there is a Minyan present—at least ten Jewish adults. That makes it very important to assemble a Minyan when there are mourners present, and being able to fill out a Minyan or say *Kaddish* for someone who is unabloe to is considered a great Mitzva (a good ded, but also a fulfillment of a commandment).

Typically, mourners stand while saying *Kaddish* every night for the first week after a close relative's death, then on the Shabbat that falls nearest the anniversary of the death every year afterward. Others remain seated, and may either say the *Kaddish*, or just recite the Amens and the middle section while the leader and mourners say it. The customs will vary from congregation to congregation, and from family to family.

The *Kaddish* is repeated several times during the service in slightly different forms. Mourners stand only for this one and the Kaddish on p. 54.

TRANSLATION

May Your holy name be honored and exalted in the world You created by Your will.

And may You rule as king over all the earth in our lifetimes, and in the lifetimes of all the families of Israel.

May that time come swiftly and soon.

And we answer, Amen.

May Your name be blessed for all the world and for all eternity.

Blessed and praised and glorified and exalted and raised up and honored and elevated and lauded is the name of the holy one, blessed are You.

You are beyond all of our blessings and songs, beyond all the praises and consolations that are spoken in all creation.

And we answer, Amen.

May your peace descend from the heavens and give renewed life to all of us and to all the land.

And we answer, Amen.

May You who spreads peace from Your heavens, bring peace to all of us, and to all the land.

And we answer, Amen.

RABBI'S KADDISH   קדיש דרבנן

MOURNERS ONLY (others say only the Amen out loud)

Yitga dal vi yitka dash shi mei ra ba   יִתְגַּדַּל וְיִתְקַדַּשׁ שְׁמֵהּ רַבָּא.
Grow exalted and be made holy Your name that is great

bi alma dee vra keeru tei   בְּעָלְמָא דִּי בְרָא כִרְעוּתֵהּ.
in the world You created according to Your will

vi yam leekh mal khutei bi kha yei khon   וְיַמְלִיךְ מַלְכוּתֵהּ בְּחַיֵּיכוֹן
and may You rule as king in our lifetimes

uvyo meikhon uvkha yei di khol beit   וּבְיוֹמֵיכוֹן וּבְחַיֵּי דְכָל בֵּית
and in our days and in the lifetimes of all the family

yisrael ba agala uveezman ko reev   יִשְׂרָאֵל בַּעֲגָלָא וּבִזְמַן קָרִיב.
of Israel swiftly and at a time that comes soon

vi eemru **amein**.   וְאִמְרוּ אָמֵן:
and we answer, Amen.

(Everyone says this part out loud)

Yi hei shmei raba mi va rakh li olam   יְהֵא שְׁמֵהּ רַבָּא מְבָרַךְ לְעָלַם
May Your name that is great be blessed for all the world

ul almei al ma ya   וּלְעָלְמֵי עָלְמַיָּא:
and for all eternity.

MOURNERS ONLY (others say only the Amens out loud)

Yeet barakh vi yeesh tabakh vi yeet ramam   יִתְבָּרַךְ וְיִשְׁתַּבַּח וְיִתְרֹמֵם
Blessed and praised and glorified and exalted

vi yeet na sei vi yeet ha dar vi yeet aleh   וְיִתְנַשֵּׂא וְיִתְהַדָּר וְיִתְעַלֶּה
and raised up and honored and elevated

vi yeet halal shi mei di kudisha, bi reekh   וְיִתְהַלָּל שְׁמֵהּ דְּקֻדְשָׁא. בְּרִיךְ
and lauded be the name of the holy one, blessed

hu, li eila meen col beerkha ta   הוּא. לְעֵלָּא מִן כָּל בִּרְכָתָא
are You. Beyond any and all blessings

vi shee ra ta tushbi khata vi nekhe mata   וְשִׁירָתָא תֻּשְׁבְּחָתָא וְנֶחֱמָתָא
and songs, praises and consolations

da ameeran bi alma, vi eemru   דַּאֲמִירָן בְּעָלְמָא. וְאִמְרוּ
that are spoken in all creation, and we answer,

amein. yi hei shlomo raba meen   אָמֵן: יְהֵא שְׁלָמָא רַבָּא מִן
Amen. May there be peace that is plentiful from

shi ma ya vi kha yeem aleinu vi al   שְׁמַיָּא וְחַיִּים עָלֵינוּ וְעַל
heaven and life upon us and upon

col yisrael, vi eemru **amein**.   כָּל־יִשְׂרָאֵל. וְאִמְרוּ אָמֵן:
all Israel, and we answer, Amen.

Oseh shalom beemro mav hu   עֹשֶׂה שָׁלוֹם בִּמְרוֹמָיו הוּא
May the one who makes peace from Your heavens, may You

ya aseh shalom aleinu vi al   יַעֲשֶׂה שָׁלוֹם עָלֵינוּ וְעַל
make peace upon us and upon

col yisrael, vi eemru **amein**.   כָּל־יִשְׂרָאֵל. וְאִמְרוּ אָמֵן:
all Israel, and we answer, Amen.

ABOUT THE PRAYER

The *Barkhu* is the call to prayer, the formal beginning of the *Maariv* (evening) service. The prayers on this page are only said if there is a *minyan* (10 adult Jews) present; otherwise, begin the service on the next page.

Traditionally, the first line of the *Barkhu* is sung by the leader of the service, and the second by the leader and the congregation together; the rest of the prayer is read silently, ending when the leader chants the last blessing out loud. Worshippers bow on each of the first two lines of the prayer.

In the days of the Temple, sacrifices were made during the day, but not at night. Anything not burned on the altar during the day would still be burned at night, so an optional service was held. After the destruction of the Temple, the service became more important, with the *Ameeda* (p. 36) replacing the role of the original sacrifices.

TRANSLATION

Praise God, who is blessed. Blessed are You, oh God, who is blessed throughout all creation. Blessed are You, oh God our lord, king of all creation, whose command brings nightfall, whose wisdom opens doors, whose understanding controls time, changes the seasons, and controls the stars in their movements through the sky as You intend. You create day and night, rolling away light so darkness can come, and darkness so light can come. You end the day and bring us night, and distinguish between day and night. God, "lord of dominions" is Your name. You live and last eternally; rule over us thoughout all creation. Blessings upon You, oh God, who brings on the night.

ALTERNATE TRANSLATION

Blessed are You, oh God of blessings,
  Ruler of all creation.
At Your command the night comes,
  Bringing us this Sabbath.

Your wisdom opens doors for us,
  Bringing us knowledge and meaning.
Your understanding gives shape to the universe
  And brings shape to our lives

You bring us the seasons, and with them
  The changes that shape our lives.
The stars move through the heavens
  In response to Your understanding.

You bring us both day and night:
  Taking the light so darkness can come,
Then taking the darkness so light can return.
  You end the day and bring us night

Oh Lord, whose dominions are endless,
  Who touches all that is and will be,
Please watch over us tonight,
  As you watch over all Your creation.

Blessed are You, oh Lord our God,
  Who brings us this night.

BARKHU

בָּרְכוּ אֶת־יְיָ הַמְבֹרָךְ:

Barkhu et Adonay, ha mi vorakh.
Praise God, who is blessed.

(everyone sings the next line out loud)

בָּרוּךְ יְיָ הַמְבֹרָךְ
לְעוֹלָם וָעֶד:

Barukh Adonay, ha mi vorakh
Blessed are You, oh God, who is blessed
li olom va ed.
throughout all creation

(read the rest of the paragraph silently)

בָּרוּךְ אַתָּה יְיָ אֱלֹהֵינוּ מֶלֶךְ
הָעוֹלָם אֲשֶׁר בִּדְבָרוֹ מַעֲרִיב
עֲרָבִים בְּחָכְמָה פּוֹתֵחַ שְׁעָרִים
וּבִתְבוּנָה מְשַׁנֶּה עִתִּים וּמַחֲלִיף
אֶת־הַזְּמַנִּים וּמְסַדֵּר אֶת־הַכּוֹכָבִים
בְּמִשְׁמְרוֹתֵיהֶם בָּרָקִיעַ כִּרְצוֹנוֹ.
בּוֹרֵא יוֹם וָלַיְלָה גּוֹלֵל אוֹר
מִפְּנֵי חֹשֶׁךְ וְחֹשֶׁךְ מִפְּנֵי אוֹר.
וּמַעֲבִיר יוֹם וּמֵבִיא לַיְלָה
וּמַבְדִּיל בֵּין יוֹם וּבֵין לָיְלָה.
יְיָ צְבָאוֹת שְׁמוֹ. אֵל חַי וְקַיָּם
תָּמִיד יִמְלוֹךְ עָלֵינוּ לְעוֹלָם וָעֶד.
בָּרוּךְ אַתָּה יְיָ הַמַּעֲרִיב עֲרָבִים:

Barukh atah Adonay, eloheinu melekh
Blessed are You, oh God our lord, king
ha olam, ah sher beed va ro ma areev
of all creation, whose command brings
ah ravim bikhakhma po tei akh shi arim
nightfall, whose wisdom opens doors,
uveetvuna mi sha ne eeteem umakhaleef
whose understanding controls time and changes
et haz ma nim umi sa deir et ha cokhavim
the seasons and controls the stars
bimeeshmiroteihem bara cee ah ceertzono.
in their movements through the sky as You intend.
Bo rei yom va lyla go leil or
You create day and night, rolling away light
meepnei khishekh vi khishekh meepnei or.
so darkness can come, and darkness so light can come.
Uma avir yom umei vee lyla
You end the day and bring us night
umavdeel bein yom uvein lyla.
and distinguish between day and between night.
Adonay tzi vah ot shimo. Eil khay vikayom
God, lord of dominions is Your name. You live and last
tamid yeemlokh aleinu li olam va ed.
eternally; rule over us thoughout all creation.
Barukh atah Adonay, ha ma ariv araveem.
Blessings upon You, oh God, who brings on the night.

TRANSLATION

You have loved Your people, Israel, with a love that will last for all of time. You have taught us Your Torah and commandments and laws and rules. Therefore, oh Lord our God, from the moment we awake until our eyes close in sleep, we will strive to absorb and understand what You have taught us. We will celebrate Your gift of the Torah and commandments for all the time given us, for in those words will we find fulfillment and sustenance for the rest of our lives. We will strive to understand Your words day and night. May your love be upon us for all of time. Blessed are You, oh God, who loves Your people, Israel.

ALTERNATE TRANSLATION

You have loved us with an eternal love.
You have taught us Your Torah
You have taught us Your commandments
You have taught us Your rules and laws.

We will learn and live by Your Torah and laws
We will make them a part of us
When we lie down and when we awaken
We will strive to absorb and understand
All that You have taught us.

We will celebrate forever Your gift to us
Of the Torah and commandments
For that gift and those words
Are our life and the the length of our days
We will strive to understand them day and night.

May your love stay with us for all of time,
And Your gift of the Torah and commandments.
Blessed are You, oh God,
Who loves your people, Israel.

אַהֲבַת עוֹלָם בֵּית יִשְׂרָאֵל עַמְּךָ
אָהַבְתָּ. תּוֹרָה וּמִצְוֹת הֻקִּים
וּמִשְׁפָּטִים אוֹתָנוּ לִמַּדְתָּ.
עַל־כֵּן יְיָ אֱלֹהֵינוּ בְּשָׁכְבֵּנוּ
וּבְקוּמֵנוּ נָשִׂיחַ בְּחֻקֶּיךָ.
וְנִשְׂמַח בְּדִבְרֵי תוֹרָתֶךָ
וּבְמִצְוֹתֶיךָ לְעוֹלָם וָעֶד.
כִּי הֵם חַיֵּינוּ וְאֹרֶךְ
יָמֵינוּ וּבָהֶם נֶהְגֶּה יוֹמָם
וָלָיְלָה. וְאַהֲבָתְךָ אַל תָּסִיר
מִמֶּנּוּ לְעוֹלָמִים.
בָּרוּךְ אַתָּה יְיָ עַמּוֹ יִשְׂרָאֵל:

Ahavat olam beit Yisra eil amkha

A love that is eternal for Israel, Your people,

ahavta. Torah u meetzvot hu keem

You have loved. Torah and commandments and laws

u meesh peh teem otahnu lee mod ta.

and rules You have taught us.

Al kein Adonay eloheinu bi shakh beinu

Therefore, oh Lord our God, before we sleep

uv cumeinu na see akh bi khu keykha

and when we awake we will absorb what You have taught us

vi nees makh bi deevrei torah tekha

and we will celebrate the words of Your Torah

u vi mitzvoteykha li olam va ed.

and Your commandments for all of creation,

Kee heim kha yeiynu vi orekh

for in those words is our life and the the length

yameinu u vahem ne hi geh yo mam

of our days, and we will strive to understand them day

va lyla. Vi ahavatkha al taseer

and night. Your love do not take away

mee mehnu li olameem

from us for all of time.

Barukh atah Adonay, amoh Yisra eil.

Blessings upon You, oh God, who loves Your people, Israel.

ABOUT THE PRAYER

The *Shima* is perhaps the most important prayer in Judaism. It is the key prayer that observant Jews say when they wake up and the last thing they say when they go to sleep. It's the last prayer you say when you're dying.

The word כָּבוֹד (ki vod) is usually translated as "glorious," but more literally means "honorable."

Orthodox and traditional Jews will wear *Tefillin*, phylacteries bound on the arm and forehead containingkey prayers on specially prepared scrolls. On folktale tells of a Jewish buisnessman who wore his Tefillin not just while worshipping, but to the marketplace as well. That way, when he shook hands with someone, he would see the *Tefillin* and be remided to do God's will.

Most Jews post a *Mezuza* on each exterior door of their houses, also containing sacred texts (sometimes still handwritten by scribes on specially prepared parchment, though cheaper versions are no longer handritten). On entering the house, you kiss your hand and touch the *Mezuza*.

TRANSLATION

Listen, O Israel! You are our God, and you are One.

(*silently*) Blessed is Your name, You who rule over all the universe.

You shall love Me with all your heart, and with all your soul, and with all your strength. And My words shall be in your heart, and you shall teach them to your children well. You shall talk of My words when you sit in your house, and when you walk down the road. They shall be the last thing you think of when you go to sleep, and the first thing you think of when you wake up. And you shall fasten those words as a reminder to your arms and between your eyes. And you shall attach My words to the doorposts of your house and to your gates.

ALTERNATE VERSION

Hear, O Israel: the Lord our God, the Lord is One.

(*silently*) Blessed be His name, whose glorious kingdom is for ever and ever.

And thou shalt love the Lord thy God with all thine heart, and with all thy soul, and with all thy might. And these words, which I command thee this day, shall be upon thine heart: and thou shalt teach them diligently unto thy children, and shall talk of them when thou sittest in thine house, and when thou walkest by the way, and when thou liest down, and when thou risest up. And thou shalt bind them for a sign upon thine hand, and they shall be for frontlets between thine eyes. And thou shalt write them upon the doorposts of thy house, and upon thy gates.
(CDP 1906)

SHI MA   שְׁמַע

(sing the first sentence loudly while covering your eyes)

Shi ma Yis ra eil
Listen and understand, Israel

שְׁמַע יִשְׂרָאֵל

Adonay eloheinu, Adonay eh khad.
God is our lord, God is one

יְהֹוָה אֱלֹהֵינוּ יְהֹוָה אֶחָד:

(say this sentence in a whisper)

Barukh sheim ki vod
Blessed is the name whose glorious

בָּרוּךְ שֵׁם כְּבוֹד

mal khuto li oh lam va ed.
kingdom is all eternity

מַלְכוּתוֹ לְעוֹלָם וָעֶד:

(sing the following together)

Vi ahavta eit Adonay eh lo heykha
You shall love God your God

וְאָהַבְתָּ אֵת יְהֹוָה אֱלֹהֶיךָ

bi khol li vav kha u vikhol naf shi kha
with all your heart, with all your soul,

בְּכָל־לְבָבְךָ וּבְכָל־נַפְשְׁךָ

u vikhol mi o dekha. Vi ha yu hadivarim
and with all your power. They should be these things

וּבְכָל־מְאֹדֶךָ: וְהָיוּ הַדְּבָרִים

ha eileh asher anokhi mitzavkha ha yom
that I command you today

הָאֵלֶּה אֲשֶׁר אָנֹכִי מְצַוְּךָ הַיּוֹם

al li va vekha. Vi shee nantam li va nekha
upon your heart. Teach them well to your children

עַל־לְבָבֶךָ: וְשִׁנַּנְתָּם לְבָנֶיךָ

vi dee barta bam bisheev tikha biveitekha
and s\talk about them while sitting in your home

וְדִבַּרְתָּ בָּם בְּשִׁבְתְּךָ בְּבֵיתֶךָ

u vi lekhtikha va derekh u vi shakh bikha
and while you walk on the road and when you lie down

וּבְלֶכְתְּךָ בַדֶּרֶךְ וּבְשָׁכְבְּךָ

uv kumekha. U kishar tam li ot
and when you rise up. Bind them as a sign

וּבְקוּמֶךָ: וּקְשַׁרְתָּם לְאוֹת

al ya dekha vi ha yu li totafot bein
upon your arm and they shall be an ornament between

עַל־יָדֶךָ וְהָיוּ לְטֹטָפֹת בֵּין

einekha. Ukhtavtam al mi zuzot
your eyes. And write them on the doorposts

עֵינֶיךָ: וּכְתַבְתָּם עַל־מְזֻזוֹת

bei tekha u vishee areykha.
of your house and on your gates.

בֵּיתֶךָ וּבִשְׁעָרֶיךָ:

(read silently until the end of p. 32 or in English on p. 32)

bam bisheevtikha biveitekha uvilekhtikha *them while you sit in your home and while you walk*	בָּם בְּשִׁבְתְּךָ בְּבֵיתֶךָ וּבְלֶכְתְּךָ
va derekh u vi shakh bikha uv kumekha. *on the road, when you lie down and when you rise up.*	בַדֶּרֶךְ וּבְשָׁכְבְּךָ וּבְקוּמֶךָ:
Ukhtavtam al mi zuzot bei tekha *And write them on the doorposts of your house*	וּכְתַבְתָּם עַל־מְזֻזוֹת בֵּיתֶךָ
u vishee arekha. Lima an yeerbu yimeikhem *and on your gates. In order to lengthen*	וּבִשְׁעָרֶיךָ: לְמַעַן יִרְבּוּ יְמֵיכֶם
yeemei vineikhem al ha adama asher *your days and the days of your children upon the land that*	וִימֵי בְנֵיכֶם עַל הָאֲדָמָה אֲשֶׁר
neeshba Adonay la avoteikhem lateit lahem *promised God to your ancestors to give them*	נִשְׁבַּע יְיָ לַאֲבֹתֵיכֶם לָתֵת לָהֶם
keemei hashamayeem al ha aretz. *like the days of heaven on the earth.*	כִּימֵי הַשָּׁמַיִם עַל־הָאָרֶץ:

NUMBERS 15:37–15:41

Va yomer Adonay el Moshe leimor dabeir *Spoke God to Moses, saying, talk*	וַיֹּאמֶר יְיָ אֶל־מֹשֶׁה לֵּאמֹר: דַּבֵּר
el binei Yisra eil vi amarta aleihem *to the people of Israel and say to them*	אֶל־בְּנֵי יִשְׂרָאֵל וְאָמַרְתָּ אֲלֵהֶם
vi asu lahem tzeetzeet al kanfei *that they are to make for themselves fringes on the corners*	וְעָשׂוּ לָהֶם צִיצִת עַל־כַּנְפֵי
beegdeihem lidorotam vinatnu al tzeetzeet *of their garments and they are to attach to the fringes*	בִגְדֵיהֶם לְדֹרֹתָם וְנָתְנוּ עַל־צִיצִת
hakanaf piteel tikheilet. Vihaya lakhem *on the corners thread of blue wool, which shall make up for you*	הַכָּנָף פְּתִיל תְּכֵלֶת: וְהָיָה לָכֶם
litzeetzeet uri eetem oto uzkhartem *the fringes and when you see them you will remember*	לְצִיצִת וּרְאִיתֶם אֹתוֹ וּזְכַרְתֶּם
et col meetzvot Adonay va aseetem otam *all the commandments of God and you will perform them*	אֶת־כָּל־מִצְוֹת יְיָ וַעֲשִׂיתֶם אֹתָם
vilo taturu akharei li vavkhem *and not follow after your heart*	וְלֹא תָתוּרוּ אַחֲרֵי לְבַבְכֶם
vi akharei eiyneiykhem asher atem zoneem *and after your eyes with which you stray*	וְאַחֲרֵי עֵינֵיכֶם אֲשֶׁר־אַתֶּם זֹנִים
akhareihem. Li ma an teezkru *after them. With these you will remember*	אַחֲרֵיהֶם: לְמַעַן תִּזְכְּרוּ
va aseetem et col meetzvotay vi hi yeetem *and perform all of my commandments and be*	וַעֲשִׂיתֶם אֶת־כָּל־מִצְוֹתָי וִהְיִיתֶם
kidosheem leiloheikhem. Anee Adonay *holy to your God. I am God*	קְדֹשִׁים לֵאלֹהֵיכֶם: אֲנִי יְיָ
eloheikhem asher hotzeitee et khem *your God, who rescud you*	אֱלֹהֵיכֶם אֲשֶׁר הוֹצֵאתִי אֶתְכֶם

DEUTERONOMY 11:13–11:21

Vihaya eem shamo ah teesh mi u *And it will be, if you always listen*	וְהָיָה אִם־שָׁמֹעַ תִּשְׁמְעוּ
el meetzvotay asher anokhee mitzaveh *to my instructions that I command*	אֶל־מִצְוֹתַי אֲשֶׁר אָנֹכִי מְצַוֶּה
etkhem hayom li ahava et Adonay *you today, to love God*	אֶתְכֶם הַיּוֹם לְאַהֲבָה אֶת־יְיָ
eloheikhem ulavdo bikhol livavkhem *your God with all your heart*	אֱלֹהֵיכֶם וּלְעָבְדוֹ בְּכָל־לְבַבְכֶם
uvikhol nafshikhem. Vinatatee *and with all your soul, then I will provide*	וּבְכָל־נַפְשְׁכֶם: וְנָתַתִּי
mi tar artzikhem bi eeto yo reh *rain for the land in its proper time, the early rain*	מְטַר־אַרְצְכֶם בְּעִתּוֹ יוֹרֶה
umalkosh vi asafta di ganekha vi teershikha *and the late rain, so you may gather your grain and your wine*	וּמַלְקוֹשׁ וְאָסַפְתָּ דְגָנֶךָ וְתִירֹשְׁךָ
vi yeetzharekha. Vi natatee eisev bi sadkha *and your oil. I will provide plants in your fields*	וְיִצְהָרֶךָ: וְנָתַתִּי עֵשֶׂב בְּשָׂדְךָ
leevhemtekha vi akhalta vi sava ita. *for your herds, and you will eat and be satisfied.*	לִבְהֶמְתֶּךָ וְאָכַלְתָּ וְשָׂבָעְתָּ:
Heeshamru lakhem pekh yeefteh li vavkhem *Take care for yourself that your heart is not seduced*	הִשָּׁמְרוּ לָכֶם פֶּן יִפְתֶּה לְבַבְכֶם
vi sartem va avadtem eloheem akhareem *and you wander astray and serve the gods of others*	וְסַרְתֶּם וַעֲבַדְתֶּם אֱלֹהִים אֲחֵרִים
viheeshtakhaveeetem lahem. Vi khara *and bow down to them. Then will burn*	וְהִשְׁתַּחֲוִיתֶם לָהֶם: וְחָרָה
af Adonay bakhem vi atzar et hashamayeem *the anger of God against you. God will hold back the skies*	אַף־יְיָ בָּכֶם וְעָצַר אֶת־הַשָּׁמַיִם
vi lo yeehiyeh matar vi ha adama lo teetein *and there will be no rain and the ground will not yield*	וְלֹא־יִהְיֶה מָטָר וְהָאֲדָמָה לֹא תִתֵּן
et yi vula va avadtem miheira mei al *any crops. And you will be banished swiftly from*	אֶת־יְבוּלָהּ וַאֲבַדְתֶּם מְהֵרָה מֵעַל
ha aretz hatova asher Adonay notein lakhem. *the land of bounty which God gives you.*	הָאָרֶץ הַטֹּבָה אֲשֶׁר יְיָ נֹתֵן לָכֶם:
vi samtem et divaray eilekh *Put these words of Mine*	וְשַׂמְתֶּם אֶת־דְּבָרַי אֵלֶּה
al livavkhem vi al nafshikhem *in your heart and in your soul.*	עַל־לְבַבְכֶם וְעַל־נַפְשְׁכֶם
ukshartem otam li ot al yedkhem *Bind them as a sign upon your arm.*	וּקְשַׁרְתֶּם אֹתָם לְאוֹת עַל־יֶדְכֶם
vi hayu li totafot bein eineikhem. *And they shall be ornaments between your eyes.*	וְהָיוּ לְטוֹטָפֹת בֵּין עֵינֵיכֶם:
Vi leemadtem otam et bi neikhem li dabeir *Teach them to your children, and talk about*	וְלִמַּדְתֶּם אֹתָם אֶת־בְּנֵיכֶם לְדַבֵּר

ABOUT THE PRAYER

The number of responsive readings may be varied depending on the needs of the congregation. Traditionally, other readings are inserted between "It is true and certain" and "Help us, O Lord" if more readers are desired, or just read these two for a shorter service. There are additional readings throughout the book.)

One custom that works well for synagogues with children is to have each child who is of reading age do a reading. That makes the children feel more involved in the service, and gets them used to standing up in front of the congragation, so a Bar or Bat Meetzvah doesn't seem quite as intimidating. Younger children can be given easier readings.

There are a number of plays on the word "true" in "It is true and certain." The morning version of the prayer starts with "true and faithful," while the evening starts with "true and certain."

הַשְׁכִּיבֵנוּ יי

This is a modern adaptation from a traditional translation of the Hebrew text. The original translation is modernized and rewritten from CDP 1906.

> Help us to lie down in peace, and to rise again in new life tomorrow. Spread the shelter of Your peace over us.

> Steer us well through Your good counsel. Save us for Your name's sake. Be a shield that surrounds us.

> Remove disease, pain, hunger, and sorrow from our lives. Remove the dangers that lurk before us and behind us.

> Shelter us beneath the shadow of Your wings. For You, Oh God, are our guardian and our deliverer.

> Guard our going out and our coming into life, Bring us into peace from this time forth and forevermore. Blessed are You, who guards Your people forever.

אֱמֶת וֶאֱמוּנָה

This is a modern adaptation from a traditional translation of the Hebrew text. The original translation is modernized and rewritten from CDP 1906, and the emphasis on divine vengeance has been toned down slightly.

> It is true and certain that You are the Lord our God, and we are your people. We follow no other God beside You.

> It is You who redeemed us from the hands of kings who oppressed us, even from our own king. It is You who delivered us from the grasp of all the terrible ones

> You dealt punishment and judgment to our adversaries when we couldnt. You requited all the enemies of our souls

> Who has performed miracles past counting? Who preserves our souls in this life and holds us steadfast in the storm. Who carries us onto the high places and exalts us over all who hated us.

> Who performed signs and wonders in the land of Egypt, and brought us forth from slavery into to everlasting freedom.

> When Your children beheld Your might, they gave thanks unto Your name, and willingly accepted Your sovereignty. Moses and the children of Israel cried out with joy, saying, Who is like unto You among the mighty ones? Who is like unto You, glorious in holiness, revered in praises, doing wonders?

> Your children beheld Your power as You split the sea before Moses. They exclaimed, This is my God! and they said, You shall reign for ever and ever.

> For the Lord has delivered Israel, and redeemed us from the hands of those whe were more powerful than we were. Blessed are You, who has redeemed Israel.

mei eretz meetzrayeem leehiyot lakhem
from the land of Egypt so I could be to you
leiloheem anee Adonay eloheinu.
to be to you a God, your God

מֵאֶרֶץ מִצְרַיִם לִהְיוֹת לָכֶם
לֵאלֹהִים אֲנִי יְיָ אֱלֹהֵיכֶם:

Adonay eloheikhem emet.
God is your God, it is true.

יְיָ אֱלֹהֵיכֶם אֱמֶת:

(read silently — continued from Shema on p. 28)

And it will come to pass, if you listen faithfully to the words that I give you today, to love your God with all your heart and with all your soul, then I will provide rain for the land when it's needed, the spring rains and the winter rains, so you may gather your grain and your wine and your oil. I will provide fodder for your herds, and you will eat and be satisfied.

But take care that your heart is not seduced by other gods. If you wander astray and serve the gods of others and bow down to them, the anger of God will burn against you. I will hold back the skies and there will be no rain, and the ground will not yield any crops. You will be banished swiftly from the fertile land which I have given you.

Put My words in your heart and in your soul. Bind them as a sign upon your arm. Wear them as ornaments between your eyes. Teach them to your children, and talk about them while you sit in your home and while you walk on the road, when you lie down at night and when you rise up in the morning. And write them on the doorposts of your house and on your gates.

If you follow My words, you will lengthen your days and the days that your children live in the land thatl promised to your ancestors. And it will be like the days of heaven on the earth.

God spoke to Moses, saying, Talk to the people of Israel and say to them that they are to make for themselves fringes on the corners of their garments, and attach blue threads to the fringes. When you see them, you will remember all of My commandments and you will perform them faithfully.

Guard your heart, and your eyes, and do not let them lead you astray. Look to the threads, and when you see them you will remember to perform all of my commandments, and to be holy to your God. I am your God, who rescued you from the land of Egypt so I could be your God.

I am your God, your true God.

HALF KADDISH

הֲצִי קַדִּישׁ

(sung by the leader)

Yitga dal vi yitka dash shi mei ra ba

יִתְגַּדַל וְיִתְקַדַּשׁ שְׁמֵהּ רַבָּא.

Grow exalted and be made holy God's name that is great

bi alma dee vra keeru tei

בְּעָלְמָא דִּי בְרָא כִרְעוּתֵהּ.

in the world God created according to God's will

vi yam leekh mal khutei bi kha yei khon

וְיַמְלִיךְ מַלְכוּתֵהּ בְּחַיֵּיכוֹן

and may God rule as king in your lifetime

uvyo meikhon uvkha yei di khol beit

וּבְיוֹמֵיכוֹן וּבְחַיֵּי דְכָל בֵּית

and in your days and in the lifetimes of all the family

yisrael ba agala uveezman ko reev

יִשְׂרָאֵל בַּעֲגָלָא וּבִזְמַן קָרִיב.

of Israel swiftly and at a time that comes soon

vi eemru amein.

וְאִמְרוּ אָמֵן:

and we answer, Amen.

(Everyone sings this part)

Yi hei shmei raba mi va rakh li olam

יְהֵא שְׁמֵהּ רַבָּא מְבָרַךְ לְעָלַם

May God's name that is great be blessed for all the world

ul almei al ma ya

וּלְעָלְמֵי עָלְמַיָּא:

and for all eternity

(sung by the leader)

Yeet barakh vi yeesh tabakh vi yeet ramam

יִתְבָּרַךְ וְיִשְׁתַּבַּח וְיִתְרֹמַם

Blessed and praised and glorified and exalted

vi yeet na sei vi yeet ha dar vi yeet aleh

וְיִתְנַשֵּׂא וְיִתְהַדָּר וְיִתְעַלֶּה

and raised up and honored and elevated

vi yeet halal shi mei di kudisha, bi reekh

וְיִתְהַלָּל שְׁמֵהּ דְּקֻדְשָׁא. בְּרִיךְ

and lauded be the name of the holy one, blessed

hu, li eila meen col beerkha ta

הוּא. לְעֵלָּא מִן כָּל בִּרְכָתָא

is He. Beyond any and all blessings

vi shee ra ta tushbi khata vi nekhe mata

וְשִׁירָתָא תֻּשְׁבְּחָתָא וְנֶחֱמָתָא

and songs, praises and consolations

da ameeran bi alma, vi eemru

דַּאֲמִירָן בְּעָלְמָא. וְאִמְרוּ

that are spoken in all creation, and we answer,

amein.

אָמֵן:

Amen.

VI SHAMRU

וְשָׁמְרוּ

(sing the following together)

Vi shamru vi nei Yisra eil et ha Shabat
And keep shall the children of Israel the Sabbath

la asot et ha Shabat li dorotam
to name the Sabbath for every generation

bi reet olam.
a covenant for all eternity.

Veiynee uvein binei Yasra eil ot hee
Between Me and between the children of Israel a sign it is

li olam kee sheishet yameem asah Adonay
that in six days God made

et hashamayeem vi et ha aretz
the skies and the land

uvayom hashveeyee Shavat vayeena fash.
and on the seventh day God rested and was refreshed.

וְשָׁמְרוּ בְנֵי־יִשְׂרָאֵל אֶת־הַשַּׁבָּת

לַעֲשׂוֹת אֶת־הַשַּׁבָּת לְדֹרֹתָם

בְּרִית עוֹלָם:

בֵּינִי וּבֵין בְּנֵי־יִשְׂרָאֵל אוֹת הִיא

לְעֹלָם כִּי־שֵׁשֶׁת יָמִים עָשָׂה יְיָ

אֶת־הַשָּׁמַיִם וְאֶת־הָאָרֶץ

וּבַיּוֹם הַשְּׁבִיעִי שָׁבַת וַיִּנָּפַשׁ:

(read this on festivals only)

vay dabeir Moshe et mo adei Adonay
Moses told of the festivals of God

el bi nei Yisrael
to the children of Israel.

וַיְדַבֵּר מֹשֶׁה אֶת־מֹעֲדֵי יְיָ

אֶל־בְּנֵי יִשְׂרָאֵל

ABOUT THE PRAYER

The Ameeda is a key prayer in the *Maariv*. It substitutes for the sacrifices to God that can no longer be made since the destruction of the Temple in Jerusalem It is perhaps the most personal prayer in the Shabbat service, but ends with a plaintive hope that the Temple might be restored in our lifetimes, so we can sacrifice to God again.

Depending on local customs, the Ameeda is sometimes all said silently, and sometimes partly sung. But either way, most of it is spent in silent prayer. (One tradition is to say the prayer in a mumble, loud enough for yourself to hear but not for others; the effect makes it sound as if the synagogue is infested with bees.) The part of the Ameeda that is someomes sung is provided in both Hebrew and English, while the silent reading is given only in English.

Just before finishing the Ameeda, you may add any personal prayers you wish.

When you begin the Ameeda, after the first sentence is sung, take three steps back (to give yourself room) and then three steps forward and bow, as if presenting yourself in a throne room. Some congragations whisper the first sentence instead.

Worshippers use a slightly different version of the Ameeda if the service occurs during a festival. On Shabat Shuva (the Sabbath that falls between Rosh Hashana and Yom Keepur), use the version on p. 41. On Khanuka, use the version on p. 43. On Shimeenee Atzeret (the day after the seventh day of Sukot), also add the sentence at the end of p. 36.

TRANSLATION

The translation of the Ameeda here and on the following pages is adapted and modernized from DPB 1914.

O Lord, open my lips and my mouth shall declare Your praise.

Blessed are You, O Lord our God and god of our forebears, God of Abraham, God of Isaac, and God of Jacob, the great, mighty, and revered God, the most high God, who bestows lovingkindness, and possesses all things; who remembers the pious deeds of our ancestors, and in love will bring a redeemer to their children's children for Your name's sake.

O King, Helper, Savior, and Shield. Blessed are You, O Lord, the Shield of Abraham.

You, O Lord, are mighty forever. You quicken the dead and have the power to save.

You cause the wind to blow and the rain to fall.

You sustain the living with lovingkindness, quicken the dead with great mercy, support the falling, heal the sick, loosen the bound, and keep Your faith to those who sleep in the dust. Who is like unto You, Lord of mighty acts? Who resembles You, O King, who kills and quickens, and causes salvation to spring forth?

Faithful are You to quicken the dead. Blessed are You, O Lord, who quickens the dead.

You are Holy and Your name is holy, and holy beings praise You daily. Blessed are You, O Lord, the holy God.

AMEEDA עֲמִידָה

(the leader sings this sentence, then pauses)

Adonay sifatay teef takh upee
Lord, my lips open so my mouth

אֲדֹנָי שְׂפָתַי תִּפְתָּח וּפִי

ya geed ti heela tekha
may exclaim Your praises.

יַגִּיד תְּהִלָּתֶךָ

(sung by the leader)

Barukh atah Adonay eloheinu veilohei
Blessed are You, God, our God and the God

בָּרוּךְ אַתָּה יְיָ אֱלֹהֵינוּ וֵאלֹהֵי

avoteinu, elohei Avraham elohei
of our forefathers, God of Abraham, God of

אֲבוֹתֵינוּ. אֱלֹהֵי אַבְרָהָם אֱלֹהֵי

Yitzkhak veilohei Yaakov, ha eil
Isaac, and God of Jacob, God

יִצְחָק וֵאלֹהֵי יַעֲקֹב. הָאֵל

ha gadol ha geebor vi ha nora eil
who is great, powerful, and magnificent, God

הַגָּדוֹל הַגִּבּוֹר וְהַנּוֹרָא אֵל

el yon, gom eil hasadeem toveem
the highest, who bestows good things that are helpful

עֶלְיוֹן. גּוֹמֵל חֲסָדִים טוֹבִים

vi konei hakol, vi zokheir khasdei avot
and creates all, who recalls the goodness of our forefathers

וְקֹנֵה הַכֹּל. וְזוֹכֵר חַסְדֵי אָבוֹת

umeivee go eil leev nei vnei khem
and brings a redeemer to the children of their children

וּמֵבִיא גוֹאֵל לִבְנֵי בְנֵיהֶם

li ma an shi mo bi ahava.
for the sake of Your name with love.

לְמַעַן שְׁמוֹ בְּאַהֲבָה:

Melekh ozeir umosheeya umagein
King, helper, saviour, and shield

מֶלֶךְ עוֹזֵר וּמוֹשִׁיעַ וּמָגֵן

Barukh atah Adonay magein Avraham.
blessed are You, God, shield of Abraham.

בָּרוּךְ אַתָּה יְיָ מָגֵן אַבְרָהָם:

Atah geebor li olam Adonay mikha yei
You are mighty forever, God who restores

אַתָּה גִּבּוֹר לְעוֹלָם אֲדֹנָי מְחַיֵּה

meiteem atah rav li hosheeya
the dead, you are very able to save

מֵתִים אַתָּה רַב לְהוֹשִׁיעַ.

(read this only on Shabats between Shimeenee Atzeret and Pesakh)

Ma sheev ha ru akh umo reed ha gashem
Who makes blow the wind and makes fall the rain.

מַשִּׁיב הָרוּחַ וּמוֹרִיד הַגָּשֶׁם:

AMEEDA (Continued from p. 38)

The translation of the Ameeda here and on the following pages is adapted and modernized from DPB 1914.

You sustain the living with lovingkindness, quicken the dead with great mercy, support the falling, heal the sick, loosen the bound, and keep Your faith to those who sleep in the dust. Who is like unto You, Lord of mighty acts? Who resembles You, O King, who kills and quickens, and causes salvation to spring forth?

Faithful are You to quicken the dead. Blessed are You, O Lord, who quickens the dead.

You are Holy and Your name is holy, and holy beings praise You daily. Blessed are You, O Lord, the holy God.

You did hallow the seventh day unto Your name, as the end of the creation of heaven and earth. You did bless it above all days, and did hallow it above all seasons. And thus it is written in Your law:

And the heaven and the earth were finished and all their host. And on the seventh day God had finished His work which He had made; and He rested on the seventh day from all His work which He had made. And God blessed the seventh day, and He hallowed it, because he rested on that day from all His work which God had created and made.

Our God and God of our forebears, accept our rest. Sanctify us by Your commandments, and grant our portion in Your law. Satisfy us with Your goodness, and gladden us with Your salvation. Purify our hearts to serve You in truth. And in Your love and favor, O Lord our God, let us inherit Your holy Sabbath. And may Israel, who hallows Your name, rest on that day. Blessed are You, O God, who hallows the Sabbath.

Accept, O Lord our God, Your people Israel and their prayer. Restore the service to the oracle of Your house. Receive in love and favor both the fire-offerings or Israel and their prayer. And may the service of Your people Israel be ever acceptable unto You.

And let our eyes behold Your return in mercy to Zion. Blessed are You, O Lord, who restores Your divine presence unto Zion.

We give thanks unto You, for You are the Lord our God and the God of our forebears for ever and ever. You are the rock of our lives, the shield of our salvation through every generation. We will give thanks unto You and declare Your praise for our lives which are committed unto Your hand, and for our souls which are in Your charge, and for Your miracles, which are daily with us, and for Your wonders and Your benefits which shape our lives at all times, evening, morning, and noon. O You who are all good, whose mercies never fail; You, merciful God whose lovingkindnesses never cease, we have ever hoped in You.

For all these things Your name, O our King, shall be continually blessed and exalted for ever and ever.

And everything that lives shall give thanks unto You forever, and shall praise Your name truly, O God, our salvation and our help. Blessed are You, O Lord, whose name is all good, and to whom we owe thanks.

Grant abundant peace unto Israel Your people forever, for You are the sovereign Lord of all peace. And may it be good in Your eyes to bless Your people Israel at all ages and at every hour with Your peace.

Blessed are You, O Lord, who blesses Your people Israel with peace.

O my God! Guard my tongue from evil and my lips from speaking deceit. And to those who would curse me, let my soul keep silent; let my soul be unto all as the dust. Open my heart to Your law, and let my soul pursue Your commandments. If any plan evil against me, make their words of no effect, and

(sung by the leader)

Mikhal keil khayeem bi khesed mi kha yei
Who sustains the living with kindness, Who restores

מְכַלְכֵּל חַיִּים בְּחֶסֶד מְחַיֵּה

meiteem bi rakha meem rabeem
the dead, with mercy plentiful

מֵתִים בְּרַחֲמִים רַבִּים.

so meikh nof leem vi ro fei kholeem
Who supports the weak, who heals the sick

סוֹמֵךְ נוֹפְלִים וְרוֹפֵא חוֹלִים

umateer asureem umkayeim
Who releases the imprisoned, and Who maintains

וּמַתִּיר אֲסוּרִים וּמְקַיֵּם

eh munato lee sheinei afar,
His faith to those who sleep in the dust.

אֱמוּנָתוֹ לִישֵׁנֵי עָפָר.

mee kamokha baal givurot
Who is like you, master of great things,

מִי כָמוֹךָ בַּעַל גְּבוּרוֹת

umee do melakh,
and who compares to You,

וּמִי דוֹמֶה לָּךְ.

melekh meimeet umikhayei
oh king, who causes death and restores life

מֶלֶךְ מֵמִית וּמְחַיֶּה

umatz mee akh yi shu ah.
and makes grow salvation.

וּמַצְמִיחַ יְשׁוּעָה:

Vi ne ehman ata lihakhot meiteem
And faithful are You to restore the dead.

וְנֶאֱמָן אַתָּה לְהַחֲיוֹת מֵתִים.

Barukh atah Adonay mikhayei ha meiteem
Blessed are You, God, who restores the dead.

בָּרוּךְ אַתָּה יְיָ מְחַיֵּה הַמֵּתִים:

(Continue silently on p. 39. On festivals, use the readings on pp. 40–43)

AMEEDA (Continued from p. 39)

frustrate their designs. Do it for the sake of Your name. Do it for the sake of Your right hand. Do it for the sake of Your holiness. Do it for the sake of Your law. In order that Your beloved ones may be delivered, O save with Your right hand and answer me.

Let the words of my mouth and the meditation of my heart be acceptable before You, O Lord, my rock and my redeemer. You who make peace in Your high places, may You make peace for us and for all Israel. And we say, Amen.

May it be Your will, O Lord our God and God of our forebesars, that the temple be speedily rebuilt in our days, and grant our portion in Your law. And there we will serve You with awe, as in the days of old, and as in ancient years. Then shall the offering of Judah and Jerusalem be pleasant unto the Lord, as in the days of old, and as in ancient years.

SHABAT SHUVA AMEEDA

The translation of the Shabat Shuva Ameeda here is adapted and modernized from DPB 1914.

O Lord, open You my lips and my mouth shall declare Your praise.

Blessed are You, O Lord our God and god of our forebears, God of Abraham, God of Isaac, and God of Jacob, the great, mighty, and revered God, the most high God, who bestows lovingkindness, and possesses all things; who remembers the pious deeds of our ancestors, and in love will bring a redeemer to their children's children for Your name's sake.

Remember us unto life, O King, who delights in life, and inscribe us in the book of life, for Your own sake, O living God.

O King, Helper, Savior, and Shield. Blessed are You, O Lord, the Shield of Abraham.

You, O Lord, are mighty forever. You quicken the dead and have the power to save.

You sustain the living with lovingkindness, quicken the dead with great mercy, support the falling, heal the sick, loosen the bound, and keep Your faith to those who sleep in the dust. Who is like unto You, Lord of mighty acts? Who resembles You, O King, who kills and quickens, and causes salvation to spring forth?

Who is like unto You, Father of mercy, who in mercy remembers Your creatures unto life?

Faithful are You to quicken the dead. Blessed are You, O Lord, who quickens the dead.

You are Holy and Your name is holy, and holy beings praise You daily. Blessed are You, O Lord, the holy King.

You did hallow the seventh day unto Your name, as the end of the creation of heaven and earth. You did bless it above all days, and did hallow it above all seasons. And thus it is written in Your law:

And the heaven and the earth were finished and all their host. And on the seventh day God had finished His work which He had made; and He rested on the seventh day from all His work which He had made. And God blessed the seventh day, and He hallowed it, because he rested on that day from all His work which God had created and made.

Our God and God of our forebears, accept our rest. Sanctify us by Your commandments, and grant our portion in Your law. Satisfy us with Your goodness, and gladden us with Your salvation. Purify our hearts to serve You in truth. And in Your love and favor, O Lord our God, let us inherit Your holy Sabbath. And may Israel, who hallows Your name, rest on that day. Blessed are You, O God, who hallows the Sabbath.

Accept, O Lord our God, Your people Israel and their prayer. Restore the service to the oracle of Your house. Receive in love and favor both the fire-offerings or Israel and their prayer. And may the service of Your people Israel be ever acceptable unto You.

And let our eyes behold Your return in mercy to Zion. Blessed are You, O Lord, who restores Your divine presence unto Zion.

We give thanks unto You, for You are the Lord our God and the God of our forebears for ever and ever. You are the rock of our lives, the shield of our salvation through every generation. We will give thanks unto You and declare Your praise for our lives which are committed unto Your hand, and for our souls which are in Your charge, and for Your miracles, which are daily with us, and for Your wonders and Your benefits which shape our lives at all times, evening, morning, and noon. O You who are all good, whose mercies never fail; You, merciful God whose lovingkindnesses never cease, we have ever hoped in You.

SHABAT SHUVA AMEEDA (Continued)

For all these things Your name, O our King, shall be continually blessed and exalted for ever and ever.

O inscribe all the children of Your covenant for a happy life.

And everything that lives shall give thanks unto You forever, and shall praise Your name truly, O God, our salvation and our help. Blessed are You, O Lord, whose name is all good, and to whom we owe thanks.

Grant abundant peace unto Israel Your people forever, for You are the sovereign Lord of all peace. And may it be good in Your eyes to bless Your people Israel at all ages and at every hour with Your peace.

In the book of life, blessing, peace, and good sustenance may we be remembered and inscribed before You, we and all Your people, for a happy life and for peace. Blessed are You, O God, who makes peace.

Blessed are You, O Lord, who blesses Your people Israel with peace.

O my God! Guard my tongue from evil and my lips from speaking deceit. And to those who would curse me, let my soul keep silent; let my soul be unto all as the dust. Open my heart to Your law, and let my soul pursue Your commandments. If any plan evil against me, make their words of no effect, and frustrate their designs. Do it for the sake of Your name. Do it for the sake of Your right hand. Do it for the sake of Your holiness. Do it for the sake of Your law. In order that Your beloved ones may be delivered, O save with Your right hand and answer me.

Let the words of my mouth and the meditation of my heart be acceptable before You, O Lord, my rock and my redeemer. You who make peace in Your high places, may You make peace for us and for all Israel. And we say, Amen.

May it be Your will, O Lord our God and God of our forebesars, that the temple be speedily rebuilt in our days, and grant our portion in Your law. And there we will serve You with awe, as in the days of old, and as in ancient years. Then shall the offering of Judah and Jerusalem be pleasant unto the Lord, as in the days of old, and as in ancient years.

KHANUKA AMEEDA

The translation of the Khanuka Ameeda here is adapted and modernized from DPB 1914.

O Lord, open You my lips and my mouth shall declare Your praise.

Blessed are You, O Lord our God and god of our forebears, God of Abraham, God of Isaac, and God of Jacob, the great, mighty, and revered God, the most high God, who bestows lovingkindness, and possesses all things; who remembers the pious deeds of our ancestors, and in love will bring a redeemer to their children's children for Your name's sake.

O King, Helper, Savior, and Shield. Blessed are You, O Lord, the Shield of Abraham.

You, O Lord, are mighty forever. You quicken the dead and have the power to save.

You sustain the living with lovingkindness, quicken the dead with great mercy, support the falling, heal the sick, loosen the bound, and keep Your faith to those who sleep in the dust. Who is like unto You, Lord of mighty acts? Who resembles You, O King, who kills and quickens, and causes salvation to spring forth?

Faithful are You to quicken the dead. Blessed are You, O Lord, who quickens the dead.

You are Holy and Your name is holy, and holy beings praise You daily. Blessed are You, O Lord, the holy God.

You did hallow the seventh day unto Your name, as the end of the creation of heaven and earth. You did bless it above all days, and did hallow it above all seasons. And thus it is written in Your law:

And the heaven and the earth were finished and all their host. And on the seventh day God had finished His work which He had made; and He rested on the seventh day from all His work which He had made. And God blessed the seventh day, and He hallowed it, because he rested on that day from all His work which God had created and made.

Our God and God of our forebears, accept our rest. Sanctify us by Your commandments, and grant our portion in Your law. Satisfy us with Your goodness, and gladden us with Your salvation. Purify our hearts to serve You in truth. And in Your love and favor, O Lord our God, let us inherit Your holy Sabbath. And may Israel, who hallows Your name, rest on that day. Blessed are You, O God, who hallows the Sabbath.

Accept, O Lord our God, Your people Israel and their prayer. Restore the service to the oracle of Your house. Receive in love and favor both the fire-offerings or Israel and their prayer. And may the service of Your people Israel be ever acceptable unto You.

And let our eyes behold Your return in mercy to Zion. Blessed are You, O Lord, who restores Your divine presence unto Zion.

We give thanks unto You, for You are the Lord our God and the God of our forebears for ever and ever. You are the rock of our lives, the shield of our salvation through every generation. We will give thanks unto You and declare Your praise for our lives which are committed unto Your hand, and for our souls which are in Your charge, and for Your miracles, which are daily with us, and for Your wonders and Your benefits which shape our lives at all times, evening, morning, and noon. O You who are all good, whose mercies never fail; You, merciful God whose lovingkindnesses never cease, we have ever hoped in You.

We thank You also for the miracles, for the redemption, for the mighty deeds and saving acts that You have performed, as well as for the wars which You waged for our forebears in days of old, at this season.

KHANUKA AMEEDA (Continued)

In the days of the Hasmonean, Mattathias son of Johannan, the high priest, and his sons, when the iniquitous power of Greece rose up against Your people Israel to make them forgetful of Your law, and to foce them to violate Your statutes and commandments, then did You in Your abundant mercy rise up for them in the time of their trouble. You pleaded their cause, You judged their suit, and You avenged their wrong. You delivered the strong into the hands of the weak, the many into the hands of the few, the impure into the hands of the pure, the wicked into the hands of the righteous, and the arrogant into the hands of those who occupied themselves with Your law. For Yourself You did make a great and holy name in Your world, and for Your people Israel You worked a great deliverance and redemption on this day. And therefore Your children came into the oracle of Your house, cleansed Your temple, purified Your sanctuary, kindled lights in Your holy courts, and appointed these eight days of Khanuka in order to give thanks and praises unto Your great name.

For all these things Your name, O our King, shall be continually blessed and exalted for ever and ever.

And everything that lives shall give thanks unto You forever, and shall praise Your name truly, O God, our salvation and our help. Blessed are You, O Lord, whose name is all good, and to whom we owe thanks.

Grant abundant peace unto Israel Your people for-ever, for You are the sovereign Lord of all peace. And may it be good in Your eyes to bless Your peo-ple Israel at all ages and at every hour with Your peace.

Blessed are You, O Lord, who blesses Your people Israel with peace.

O my God! Guard my tongue from evil and my lips from speaking deceit. And to those who would curse me, let my soul keep silent; let my soul be unto all as the dust. Open my heart to Your law, and let my soul pursue Your commandments. If any plan evil against me, make their words of no effect, and frustrate their designs. Do it for the sake of Your name. Do it for the sake of Your right hand. Do it for the sake of Your holiness. Do it for the sake of Your law. In order that Your beloved ones may be delivered, O save with Your right hand and answer me.

Let the words of my mouth and the meditation of my heart be acceptable before You, O Lord, my rock and my redeemer. You who make peace in Your high places, may You make peace for us and for all Israel. And we say, Amen.

May it be Your will, O Lord our God and God of our forebesars, that the temple be speedily rebuilt in our days, and grant our portion in Your law. And there we will serve You with awe, as in the days of old, and as in ancient years. Then shall the offering of Judah and Jerusalem be pleasant unto the Lord, as in the days of old, and as in ancient years.

ABOUT THE PRAYER

This is the priestly benediction; there are several other prayers specifically for children as well. If there are a number of small children, one custom is to have them come up to the leader, who holds out his or her Tallit like a sheltering canopy over the children's heads while reciting the blessing. Another custom is to have the parents of the children touch their children on the head while the prayer is recited, so the parents themselves are blessing the children, as well as asking God's blessing on them.

TRANSLATION

May the Lord bless you and keep you.

   So may it be His will.

May the Lord make His countenance to shine on you and bring grace to you.

   So may it be His will.

May the Lord turn His countenance to shine on you and bring you peace.

   So may it be His will.

PRAYER FOR THE CHILDREN   יברכך

(leader)

Yi va rekhikha Adonay vi yeesh mi rekha
Bless you God and keep you

יְבָרֶכְךָ יְיָ וְיִשְׁמְרֶךָ.

(congregation)

Kein yi hee ratzon
Yes your will let it be

כֵּן יְהִי רָצוֹן:

(leader)

Ya eir Adonay panayv eileykha veehunekha
May God look toward you and shine to you and be gracious to you

יָאֵר יְיָ פָּנָיו אֵלֶיךָ וִיחֻנֶּךָ.

(congregation)

Kein yi hee ratzon
Yes your will let it be

כֵּן יְהִי רָצוֹן:

(leader)

Yeesa Adonay panayv eileykha vi yaseim
My God look toward you and give
likha shalom
to you peace

יִשָּׂא יְיָ פָּנָיו אֵלֶיךָ וְיָשֵׂם
לְךָ לְדִשָׁלוֹם.

(congregation)

Kein yi hee ratzon
Yes your will let it be

כֵּן יְהִי רָצוֹן:

LI KHEE LAKH

L'khi lakh, to a land that I will show you.
Leikh l'kha, to a place you do not know
L'khi lakh, on your journey I will bless you,
And (you shall be a blessing) (3x) l'khi lakh.

L'khi lakh, and I shall make your name great.
Leikh l'kha, and all shall praise your name.
L'khi lakh, to the place that I will show you.

L'sim-khat cha-yim (3x) l'khi lakh.

...AND THE YOUTH SHALL SEE VISIONS

Chorus:

And the old shall dream dream
    and the youth shall see visions,
And our hopes shall rise up to the sky.
We must live for today, we must build for tomorrow.
Give us time, give us strength, give us life.

Childhood was for fantasies, for nursery rhymes and
    toys.
The world was much too busy
    to understand small girls and boys.
As I grew up, I came to learn that life was not a
    game,
That heroes were just people that we called another
    name.

(Chorus)

Now I'm grown, the years have passed,
    I've come to understand.
There are choices to be made and my life's at my
    command.
I cannot have a future, 'til I embrace my past.
I promise to pursue the challenge, time is going fast.

(Chorus)

Today's the day we (I) take our (my) stand, the future's
    ours (mine) to hold.
Commitments that we (I) make today are dreams from
    days of old.
We'll (I) have to make the way for generations come
    and go.
We'll (I'll) have to teach them what we've (I've)
    learned
    so they will come to know:

That the old shall dream dreams.....

MEE SHEBEIRAKH

A *Mee Shebeirakh* is a traditional prayer for healing. People in the congregation can say the names of those in need of healing before the prayer is said. In recent years, the version of the *Mee Shebeirakh* here, which was written and popularized by folksinger Debbie Friedman has taken the place of the traditional prayer for many congregations.

Mee she-bei-rach a-vo-tei-nu
Mi-kor ha-bra-cha li-ee-mo-tei-nu,
May the source of strength
Who blessed the ones before us,
Help us find the courage
To make our lives a blessing,
And let us say, Amen.

Mee she-bei-rach ee-mo-tei-nu
Mi-kor ha-bra-cha li-a-vo-tei-nu,
Bless those in need of healing
With ri-fu-a sh'lei-ma,
The renewal of body,
The renewal of spirit,
And let us say, Amen.

LIKE MIRIAM

Let me be strong, like Miriam
Let me be holy, like Miriam
Let me make the world better.

> Let me be courageous, like Miriam
> Who risked her own life for her brother's
> sake.

Let me be creative, like Miriam
Who wrote songs of celebration at the Red Sea.

> Let me be loving, like Miriam
> Who gave equally to her family and to her
> people.

Let me be clever, like Miriam
Who convinced Pharaoh's daughter to take in her
brother.

> Let me be tolerant, like Miriam
> Who overcame her prejudice with God's
> help.

Let me be wise, like Miriam
Who was chosen by God as a prophet.

> Let me be nurturing, like Miriam
> Who brought water to the desert.

Let me be joyful in life, like Miriam
Who led the dancing at the seaside.

> Let me be strong, like Miriam
> Let me be holy, like Miriam
> Let me make the world better.

ABOUT THE PRAYER

Ein Adeer is a traditional Sephardic folk song that remains tremendously popular, especially with children. The song starts slowly, but speeds up with each verse and chorus, so that the congregation is racing through it by the end of the song.

Amram was the father of Moses, Aaron, and Miriam, and the wife of Jochabed.

TRANSLATION

None is as mighty as the Lord.
None is as blessed as Amram's son.
Nothing is as great as the Torah.
None understand it as Israel does.

From the mouth of God, the mouth of God
Let all Israel be blessed.

None is as glorious as the Lord.
None is as devout as Amram's son.
Nothing is as pure as the Torah.
None is as wise as Israel.

From the mouth of God, the mouth of God
Let all Israel be blessed.

None is as pure as the Lord.
None is as matchless as Amram's son.
Nothing is as mighty as the Torah.
None is as learned as Israel.

From the mouth of God, the mouth of God
Let all Israel be blessed.

None can redeem like the Lord.
None is as righteous as Amram's son.
Nothing is as holy as the Torah.
None is as steadfast as Israel.

From the mouth of God, the mouth of God
Let all Israel be blessed.

EIN ADEER | אין אדיר

Ein adeer ka Adonay
None is as mighty as the Lord

vi ein barukh ki ven Amram
None is as blessed as Amram's son

ein gidola ka Torah
Nothing is as great as the Torah

vi ein darsha neykha ki Yisra eil.
None understand it as Israel does.

Mee pee eil umee pee eil (chorus)
From the mouth of God, the mouth of God

yi vorakh col Yisra eil
Let all Israel be blessed.

אֵין אַדִּיר כַּיְיָ
וְאֵין בָּרוּךְ כְּבֶן עַמְרָם.
אֵין גְּדוֹלָה כַּתּוֹרָה
וְאֵין דַּרְשָׁנֶיהָ כְּיִשְׂרָאֵל:

מִפִּי אֵל וּמִפִּי אֵל
יְבָרֵךְ כָּל יִשְׂרָאֵל:

Ein hadur ka Adonay
None is as glorious as the Lord

vi ein vateek ki ven Amram
None is as devout as Amram's son

ein za ka ka Torah
Nothing is as pure as the Torah

vi ein khakha meykha ki Yisra eil.
None is as wise as Israel.

(chorus)

אֵין הָדוּר כַּיְיָ
וְאֵין וָתִיק כְּבֶן עַמְרָם.
אֵין זַכָּה כַּתּוֹרָה
וְאֵין חֲכָמֶיהָ כְּיִשְׂרָאֵל:

Ein adeer ka Adonay
None is as pure as the Lord

vi ein barukh ki ven Amram
None is as matchless as Amram's son

ein gidola ka Torah
Nothing is as mighty as the Torah

vi ein lamda neykha ki Yisra eil.
None is as learned as Israel.

(chorus)

אֵין טָהוֹר כַּיְיָ
וְאֵין יָחִיד כְּבֶן עַמְרָם.
אֵין כַּבִּירָה כַּתּוֹרָה
וְאֵין לַמְדָנֶיהָ כְּיִשְׂרָאֵל:

Ein adeer ka Adonay
None can redeem like the Lord

vi ein barukh ki ven Amram
None is as righteous as Amram's son

ein gidola ka Torah
Nothing is as holy as the Torah

vi ein to mi kheykha ki Yisra eil.
None is as steadfast as Israel.

(chorus)

אֵין פּוֹדֶה כַּיְיָ
וְאֵין צַדִּיק כְּבֶן עַמְרָם.
אֵין קְדוֹשָׁה כַּתּוֹרָה
וְאֵין תּוֹמְכֶיהָ כְּיִשְׂרָאֵל:

ABOUT THE PRAYER

The *Kadish Shalom* (full Kaddish) is chanted by the leader, with the congregation remaining seated. Mourners do not stand for this version of the Kaddish. The indented part is chanted by the full congregation; otherwise worshippers just echo the Amens.

After the *Kadish Shalom*, the service continues with the Aleinu. There is no Torah reading during the Friday night serivce, but if the congregation has a Torah, all stand and the ark is opened. The Torah is uncovered, but not brought out. The opening section of the Aleinu is sung, and the rest read silently. (There's a translation on this page.) When everyone is done reading, the last sentence is sung together. Then the ark is closed and everyone is seated.

ALEINU TRANSLATION

It is our duty to praise the master of everything and to acknowledge the greatness of the maker of the universe. For You have made us distinct from the peoples of other lands. You have not made us like other familes of the land. The portion you gave us was different than theirs, nor is our destiny the same as all other peoples.

We bend our knees, bow and give thanks before the king of kings of kings, the holy One, blessed are You.

You stretched out the sky and created the land. The seat of Your power is in the heavens above, and Your power reaches the most towering heights. You are our God and there is no other. You are our king, and there is no other equal to You. As it is written in Your Torah: we are to know this day and take into our hearts that You are the God in the skies above and on the land below. There is no other.

Therefore we place our hope in You, our God, that we may see soon the glory of Your power to remove worship of idols from the land. False gods will be completely eradicated, and all creation will be sanctified through the rule of the Almighty. Then all people will call Your name, and all the wicked of the land will turn toward You and beg forgiveness. May all the peoples of the world recognize and know that to You should bend every kneee, to You should swear every tongue. Before You, our God, they will bow and abase themselves. To the glory of Your name they will offer homage, and all will accept the yoke of Your kingship. May You rule over all the peoples of the earth quickly, and may Your rule last forever and ever.

For the kingdom is Yours, and forever and ever You will rule in glory, as it is written in Your Torah: God will rule forever and ever. And it is said, then will You be King of all the land, on that day shall You be one and Your name shall be one.

Yitga dal vi yitka dash shi mei ra ba
Grow exalted and be made holy Your name that is great

יִתְגַּדַּל וְיִתְקַדַּשׁ שְׁמֵהּ רַבָּא.

bi alma dee vra keeru tei
in the world You created according to Your will

בְּעָלְמָא דִּי בְרָא כִרְעוּתֵהּ.

vi yam leekh mal khutei bi kha yei khon
and may You rule as king in our lifetime

וְיַמְלִיךְ מַלְכוּתֵהּ בְּחַיֵּיכוֹן

uvyo meikhon uvkha yei di khol beit
and in our days and in the lifetimes of all the family

וּבְיוֹמֵיכוֹן וּבְחַיֵּי דְכָל בֵּית

yisrael ba agala uveezman ko reev
of Israel swiftly and at a time that comes soon

יִשְׂרָאֵל בַּעֲגָלָא וּבִזְמַן קָרִיב.

vi eemru **amein**.
and we answer, Amen.

וְאִמְרוּ אָמֵן:

Yi hei shmei raba mi va rakh li olam
May Your name that is great be blessed for all the world

יְהֵא שְׁמֵהּ רַבָּא מְבָרַךְ לְעָלַם

ul almei al ma ya
and for all eternity

וּלְעָלְמֵי עָלְמַיָּא:

Yeet barakh vi yeesh tabakh vi yeet ramam
Blessed and praised and glorified and exalted

יִתְבָּרַךְ וְיִשְׁתַּבַּח וְיִתְרוֹמַם

vi yeet na sei vi yeet ha dar vi yeet aleh
and raised up and honored and elevated

וְיִתְנַשֵּׂא וְיִתְהַדָּר וְיִתְעַלֶּה

vi yeet halal shi mei di kudisha, bi reekh
and lauded be the name of the holy one, blessed

וְיִתְהַלָּל שְׁמֵהּ דְּקֻדְשָׁא. בְּרִיךְ

hu, li eila meen col beerkha ta
are You. Beyond any and all blessings

הוּא. לְעֵלָּא מִן כָּל בִּרְכָתָא

vi shee ra ta tushbi khata vi nekhe mata
and songs, praises and consolations

וְשִׁירָתָא תֻּשְׁבְּחָתָא וְנֶחֱמָתָא

da ameeran bi alma, vi eemru
that are spoken in all creation, and we answer,

דַּאֲמִירָן בְּעָלְמָא. וְאִמְרוּ

amein . Teetka beil tzilot hon
Amen. May You accept the prayers

אָמֵן: תִּתְקַבֵּל צְלוֹתְהוֹן

uva uthon di khol Yisra eil
and pleas of all the people of Israel

וּבָעוּתְהוֹן דְּכָל־יִשְׂרָאֵל קֳדָם

avuhon dee veeshmaya, vi eemru **amein**.
before their Father who is in heaven and we answer, Amen.

אֲבוּהוֹן דִּי בִשְׁמַיָּא. וְאִמְרוּ אָמֵן:

Yi hei shlomo raba meen
Amen. May there be peace that is plentiful from

יְהֵא שְׁלָמָא רַבָּא מִן

shi ma ya vi kha yeem aleinu vi al
heaven and life upon us and upon

שְׁמַיָּא וְחַיִּים עָלֵינוּ וְעַל

col yisrael, vi eemru **amein**.
all Israel, and we answer, Amen.

כָּל־יִשְׂרָאֵל. וְאִמְרוּ אָמֵן:

Oseh shalom beemro mav hu
May the one who makes peace from Your heavens, may You

עֹשֶׂה שָׁלוֹם בִּמְרוֹמָיו הוּא

ya aseh shalom aleinu vi al
make peace upon us and upon

יַעֲשֶׂה שָׁלוֹם עָלֵינוּ וְעַל

col yisrael, vi eemru **amein**.
all Israel, and we answer, Amen.

כָּל־יִשְׂרָאֵל. וְאִמְרוּ אָמֵן:

(read silently, continued from p. 52 or in English on p. 51)

Al col ni kaveh likha Adonay eloheinu   עַל־כָּל נְקַוֶּה לְךָ יְיָ אֱלֹהֵינוּ
Therefore we place our hope in You, God our God

li ri ot mi heira bi teeferet uzekha   לִרְאוֹת מְהֵרָה בְּתִפְאֶרֶת עֻזֶּךָ
that we may see soon the glory of Your power

li ha aveer geeluleem meen ha aretz   לְהַעֲבִיר גִּלּוּלִים מִן הָאָרֶץ
to remove worship of idols from the land

vi ha eleeleem karot yeekareitun, li takein   וְהָאֱלִילִים כָּרוֹת יִכָּרֵתוּן. לְתַקֵּן
and false gods will be completely eradicated, to perfect

olam bimalkhut shaday, vi col binei   עוֹלָם בְּמַלְכוּת שַׁדַּי. וְכָל־בְּנֵי
all creation through the rule of the Almighty. Then all people

vashar yeek ri u veeshmekha li hafnot   בָשָׂר יִקְרְאוּ בִשְׁמֶךָ לְהַפְנוֹת
will call Your name to turn

eileiykha col reeshay aretz, yakeeru   אֵלֶיךָ כָּל־רִשְׁעֵי אָרֶץ. יַכִּירוּ
toward You all the wicked of the land. May they recognize

vi yeidu col yoshveiy teiveil, kee likha   וְיֵדְעוּ כָּל־יוֹשְׁבֵי תֵבֵל. כִּי־לְךָ
and know all the peoples of the world that to You

teekhra col berekh teeshava   תִּכְרַע כָּל־בֶּרֶךְ תִּשָּׁבַע
should bend every kneee

col lashon. li faneiykha Adonay eloheinu   כָּל־לָשׁוֹן: לְפָנֶיךָ יְיָ אֱלֹהֵינוּ
should swear every tongue. Before You, God our God

yeekhri u vi yeepolu, vi leekhbod sheemkha   יִכְרְעוּ וְיִפֹּלוּ. וְלִכְבוֹד שִׁמְךָ
they will bow and abase themselves and to the glory of Your name

yi kar yeeteinu, veekablu kulam et ol   יְקָר יִתֵּנוּ. וִיקַבְּלוּ כֻלָּם אֶת עוֹל
homage they will offer and accept will all the yoke

malkhutekha, vi teemlokh aleihem   מַלְכוּתֶךָ. וְתִמְלוֹךְ עֲלֵיהֶם
of Your kingship, that You may rule over them

mi heira li olam va ed, kee hamalkhut   מְהֵרָה לְעוֹלָם וָעֶד. כִּי הַמַּלְכוּת
very soon, forever and ever

shelkha hee ulolimei ad teemlokh   שֶׁלְּךָ הִיא וּלְעוֹלְמֵי עַד תִּמְלוֹךְ
for the kingdom is Yours, and forever and ever You will rule

bi khavod. kakatuv bi toratekha Adonay   בְּכָבוֹד: כַּכָּתוּב בְּתוֹרָתֶךָ יְיָ
in glory, as it is written in Your Torah: God

yeemlokh li olam va ed.   יִמְלֹךְ לְעוֹלָם וָעֶד:
will rule forever and ever.

(sing together)

Vi ne emar vi haya Adonay li melekh   וְנֶאֱמַר וְהָיָה יְיָ לְמֶלֶךְ
And it is said, then will God be king

al col ha aretz ba yom hahu   עַל־כָּל־הָאָרֶץ בַּיּוֹם הַהוּא
of all the land, on that day

yi hee ye Adonay ekhad ushmo ekhad.   יִהְיֶה יְיָ אֶחָד וּשְׁמוֹ אֶחָד:
shall Giod be one and God's name be one.

<table>
<tr><td>

ALEINU

</td><td>

עָלֵינוּ

</td></tr>
</table>

(sung by all)

<table>
<tr><td>

Aleinu li shabei akh la adon hakol
It is our duty to praise the master of everything

la teit gidula liyotzeir vi reisheet
to acknowledge the greatness of the maker of the universe

shelo asanu ki goyeiy ha ratzot
for God has not made us like the peoples of other lands

vi lo samanu ki meesh pikhot ha adama
and has not made us like other familes of the land

shelo sam khelkeinu kahem
for God has not given our portion like theirs

vi goraleinu kikhol hamonam.
nor is our destiny like that of all other peoples.

</td><td>

עָלֵינוּ לְשַׁבֵּחַ לַאֲדוֹן הַכֹּל

לָתֵת גְּדֻלָּה לְיוֹצֵר בְּרֵאשִׁית

שֶׁלֹּא עָשָׂנוּ כְּגוֹיֵי הָאֲרָצוֹת

וְלֹא שָׂמָנוּ כְּמִשְׁפְּחוֹת הָאֲדָמָה

שֶׁלֹּא שָׂם חֶלְקֵנוּ כָּהֶם

וְגֹרָלֵנוּ כְּכָל הֲמוֹנָם:

</td></tr>
</table>

(bow while this is sung)

<table>
<tr><td>

Va nakhnu koreem
But we bend our knees

umeesh takha veem umodeem
bow and give our thanks

leefnei melekh makhhei hamlakheem
before the king of kings of kings

ha kadosh barukh hoo,
the holy one, blessed is God.

</td><td>

וַאֲנַחְנוּ כּוֹרְעִים

וּמִשְׁתַּחֲוִים וּמוֹדִים

לִפְנֵי מֶלֶךְ מַלְכֵי הַמְּלָכִים

הַקָּדוֹשׁ בָּרוּךְ הוּא.

</td></tr>
</table>

(sung by all)

<table>
<tr><td>

Shehu no tei shamayeem vi yoseid aretz
God stretches out the sky and creates the land

umoshav yi karo ba shamayim meema al
the seat of God's power is in the heavens above

uvshkheen at uzo bi gavhei mi romeem.
and the presence of God's power is in the most towering heights.

Hu aloheinu ein od.
God is our God and there is no other

emet malkeinu efes zulato
It is true God is our king, there is no other equal to God

kakatuv bi torato vi yadata ha yom
as it is written in God's Torah: you are to know this day

vi hasheivota el li vavekha
and take into your heart

kee Adonay hu ha eloheem
that God is the God

ba sha mayeem mee ma al vi al ha aretz
in the skies above and on the land below

mee takhat, Ein od.
there is no other.

</td><td>

שֶׁהוּא נוֹטֶה שָׁמַיִם וְיוֹסֵד אָרֶץ

וּמוֹשַׁב יְקָרוֹ בַּשָּׁמַיִם מִמַּעַל

וּשְׁכִינַת עֻזּוֹ בְּגָבְהֵי מְרוֹמִים:

הוּא אֱלֹהֵינוּ אֵין עוֹד.

אֱמֶת מַלְכֵּנוּ אֶפֶס זוּלָתוֹ

כַּכָּתוּב בְּתוֹרָתוֹ וְיָדַעְתָּ הַיּוֹם

וַהֲשֵׁבֹתָ אֶל לְבָבֶךָ

כִּי יְיָ הוּא הָאֱלֹהִים

בַּשָּׁמַיִם מִמַּעַל וְעַל־הָאָרֶץ

מִתָּחַת. אֵין עוֹד:

</td></tr>
</table>

ALTERNATE VERSION

And now, I pray thee, let the power of the Lord be great, according as Thou hast spoken. Remember, O Lord, Thy tender mercies and Thy lovingkindness; for they have been ever of old.

Magnified and sanctified be His great name in the world which He hath created according to His will. May He establish His kingdom during your life and during your days, and during the life of all the house of Israel, even speedily and at a near time, and say ye, Amen.

Let His great name be blesses for ever and ever to all eternity.

Blessed, praised, and glorified, exalted, extolled, and honored maginified and lauded be the name of the Holy One, blessed be He; though He be high above all the blessings and hymns, praises and consolations, which are uttered in the world; and say ye, Amen.

Let the name of the Lord be blessed from this time forth and for forevermore.

May there be abundant peace from heaven, and life for us and for all Israel; and say ye, Amen.

My help is from the Lord, who made heaven and earth.

He who maketh peace in His high places may he make peace for us and for all Israel; and say ye, Amen. (DPB 1914)

TRANSLATION

May Your holy name be honored and exalted in the world You created by Your will.

And may You rule as king over all the earth in our lifetimes, and in the lifetimes of all the families of Israel.

May that time come swiftly and soon.

And we answer, Amen.

May Your name be blessed for all the world and for all eternity.

Blessed and praised and glorified and exalted and raised up and honored and elevated and lauded is the name of the holy one, blessed are You.

You are beyond all of our blessings and songs, beyond all the praises and consolations that are spoken in all creation.

And we answer, Amen.

May your peace descend from the heavens and give renewed life to all of us and to all the land.

And we answer, Amen.

May You who spreads peace from Your heavens, bring peace to all of us, and to all the land.

And we answer, Amen.

MOURNER'S KADDISH   קדיש

MOURNERS ONLY (others say only the Amen out loud)

Yitga dal vi yitka dash shi mei ra ba
Grow exalted and be made holy Your name that is great

יִתְגַּדַּל וְיִתְקַדַּשׁ שְׁמֵהּ רַבָּא.

bi alma dee vra keeru tei
in the world You created according to Your will

בְּעָלְמָא דִּי בְרָא כִרְעוּתֵהּ.

vi yam leekh mal khutei bi kha yei khon
and may You rule as king in our lifetime

וְיַמְלִיךְ מַלְכוּתֵהּ בְּחַיֵּיכוֹן

uvyo meikhon uvkha yei di khol beit
and in our days and in the lifetimes of all the family

וּבְיוֹמֵיכוֹן וּבְחַיֵּי דְכָל בֵּית

yisrael ba agala uveezman ko reev
of Israel swiftly and at a time that comes soon

יִשְׂרָאֵל בַּעֲגָלָא וּבִזְמַן קָרִיב.

vi eemru **amein**.
and we answer, Amen.

וְאִמְרוּ אָמֵן:

(Everyone says this part out loud)

Yi hei shmei raba mi va rakh li olam
May Your name that is great be blessed for all the world

יְהֵא שְׁמֵהּ רַבָּא מְבָרַךְ לְעָלַם

ul almei al ma ya
and for all eternity

וּלְעָלְמֵי עָלְמַיָּא:

MOURNERS ONLY (others say only the Amens out loud)

Yeet barakh vi yeesh tabakh vi yeet ramam
Blessed and praised and glorified and exalted

יִתְבָּרַךְ וְיִשְׁתַּבַּח וְיִתְרַמַם

vi yeet na sei vi yeet ha dar vi yeet aleh
and raised up and honored and elevated

וְיִתְנַשֵּׂא וְיִתְהַדַּר וְיִתְעַלֶּה

vi yeet halal shi mei di kudisha, bi reekh
and lauded be the name of the holy one, blessed

וְיִתְהַלָּל שְׁמֵהּ דְּקֻדְשָׁא. בְּרִיךְ

hu, li eila meen col beerkha ta
are You. Beyond any and all blessings

הוּא. לְעֵלָּא מִן כָּל בִּרְכָתָא

vi shee ra ta tushbi khata vi nekhe mata
and songs, praises and consolations

וְשִׁירָתָא תֻּשְׁבְּחָתָא וְנֶחֱמָתָא

da ameeran bi alma, vi eemru
that are spoken in all creation, and we answer,

דַּאֲמִירָן בְּעָלְמָא. וְאִמְרוּ

amein . yi hei shlomo raba meen
Amen. May there be peace that is plentiful from

אָמֵן: יְהֵא שְׁלָמָא רַבָּא מִן

shi ma ya vi kha yeem aleinu vi al
heaven and life upon us and upon

שְׁמַיָּא וְחַיִּים עָלֵינוּ וְעַל

col yisrael, vi eemru **amein**.
all Israel, and we answer, Amen.

כָּל־יִשְׂרָאֵל. וְאִמְרוּ אָמֵן:

Oseh shalom beemro mav hu
May the one who makes peace from Your heavens, may You

עֹשֶׂה שָׁלוֹם בִּמְרוֹמָיו הוּא

ya aseh shalom aleinu vi al
make peace upon us and upon

יַעֲשֶׂה שָׁלוֹם עָלֵינוּ וְעַל

col yisrael, vi eemru **amein**.
all Israel, and we answer, Amen.

כָּל־יִשְׂרָאֵל. וְאִמְרוּ אָמֵן:

YOU WHO LIVE IN THE SHELTER

This is a modern adaptation from Psalm 91. The psalm is sometimes said as a part of the evening prayers, and as a part of the prayer said before going on a journey. As with many psalms, this one relates two disconnected themes. This reading draws from the part which deals with journeys and hope and God's love, while omitting a middle passage in which the traveler witnesses God's retribution.

We who live in the shelter of the Most High, will find peace within the shadow of the Almighty. You are my refuge and my fortress, my God in whom I trust.

For You shall deliver me from the snare of the fowler, and from those who would prey on me. You shall cover me with Your pinions, and under Your wings will I take refuge.

Your truth shall be a shield that defends me. I shall not fear the terror by night, nor the arrow that flies by day; not the fever that walks in darkness, nor the plague that ravages at noon.

You have made the most high your dwelling place. There, no evil shall befall me, nor shall any scourge come into your home. For You shall send your angels to watch over me and keep me on the path. They will steady my legs if I stumble, and carry me if I fall.

Because you have set your love upon Me, therefore will I deliver you. I will set you on high, because you know My name. When you call upon Me I will answer you. I will be with you in your troubles; I will deliver and honor you. I will give you long life, and you will come to see My salvation.

ABOUT THE PRAYER

Adon Olam is one of two different songs that traditionally end the Friday night Sabbath service. (Yigdal is the other.) Congregations use one or the other.

One of the fascinating things about Adon Olam is that it can be sung to so many different tunes; While there are several more common tunes, congregations may vary tunes from week to week or stick with a favorite version. (One particulary haunting version was sung to the theme song from M*A*S*H.)

There's a tradition in our local synagogue of having one of the children at the service pick that week's tune. It's another way to get kids involved in the service and make them feel like significant participants, not just afterthoughts.

The first verse is sometimes used as a chorus between subsequent verses.

TRANSLATION

Master of everything, who was king
Before the beginning of creation.
Whose will created all things
We proclaim you our king and master.

After the end of everything
You alone will reign supreme.
You have always been, and You are now
And You always will be glorious.

You are the first and there is no second
that can compare with You or be Your equal.
You are without beginning and without end
Yours is the power and yours is the kingdom.

You are my God, my living saviour
You are the rock I cling to in times of suffering.
You are my flag, and a shelter for me
You are my sustenance and the last thing I will taste.

Into your hand I place my soul
When I go to sleep I know I shall awaken.
You protect my soul while my body sleeps
While You are with me, I have no fear.

ADON OLAM   אדון עולם

Adon olam asher ma lakh
Master of everything, who was king
Bi tehrem col yi tzeer neevra.
before anything was created.
Li eit na ah sa vi khef tzo col
At the time when Your will created all things
Ah zahy melekh shi mo neevra.
then as king Your name was proclaimed.

Vi akharei keekhlot hacol
After the end of everything
Li vado yeemlokh nora.
You alone will reign supreme.
Vi hu haya vi hu hoveh
It is You who was and You who are
Vi hu yeehiyeh bi teefara.
and You who will always be glorious.

      (chorus)

Vi hu ekhad vi ein sheinee
You are first and there is no second
Li hamsheel lo li hakhbeera.
that can compare with You or be Your equal.
Bi lee reisheet bi lee takhleet
without beginning without end
Vi lo ha oz vi ha meesra.
Yours is the power and the kingdom.

      (chorus)

Vi hu eilee vi kheiy go alee
You are my God, my living saviour
Vi tzor khevlee bi eit tzara.
a rock my pain in time of suffering.
Vi hu neesee umanos lee
You are my flag, a shelter for me
Mi nat kosee bi yom ekra.
the drink in my cup on the day I call.

      (chorus)

Bi yado afkeer rukhee
Into your hand I place my soul
Bi eit eeshan vi a eera
when I go to sleep and I shall awaken.
Vi eem rutee gi ree atee
With my soul my body shall remain
Adonay lee vi lo eera
God is with me I shall not fear.

אֲדוֹן עוֹלָם אֲשֶׁר מָלַךְ
בְּטֶרֶם כָּל יְצִיר נִבְרָא:
לְעֵת נַעֲשָׂה בְחֶפְצוֹ כֹּל
אֲזַי מֶלֶךְ שְׁמוֹ נִקְרָא:

וְאַחֲרֵי כִּכְלוֹת הַכֹּל
לְבַדּוֹ יִמְלוֹךְ נוֹרָא:
וְהוּא הָיָה וְהוּא הֹוֶה
וְהוּא יִהְיֶה בְּתִפְאָרָה:

וְהוּא אֶחָד וְאֵין שֵׁנִי
לְהַמְשִׁיל לוֹ לְהַחְבִּירָה:
בְּלִי רֵאשִׁית בְּלִי תַכְלִית
וְלוֹ הָעֹז וְהַמִּשְׂרָה:

וְהוּא אֵלִי וְחַי גוֹאֲלִי
וְצוּר חֶבְלִי בְּעֵת צָרָה:
וְהוּא נִסִּי וּמָנוֹס לִי
מְנָת כּוֹסִי בְּיוֹם אֶקְרָא:

בְּיָדוֹ אַפְקִיד רוּחִי
בְּעֵת אִישָׁן וְאָעִירָה:
וְעִם רוּחִי גְּוִיָּתִי
יְיָ לִי וְלֹא אִירָא:

ABOUT THE PRAYER

While the Keedush, the blessing over wine, actually occurs during the service, many congregations hold it after the service, before a meal or snack is served. In addition to the Keedush, the prayer over bread should be said before serving any Sabbath Khalla (a specially braided and glazed bread usually served on Shabbat) or other bread.

TRANSLATION

Blessed are You, oh God our lord, king of all creation, who creates the fruit of the vine. Blessed are You, oh God our lord, king of all creation whose commandments make us holy and who was pleased with us and with Your Sabbath, which is made holy by Your love and with Your favor. You gave us as a heritage a remembrance of the labor of creation for it is the day that comes before gatherings of holiness in remembrance of the flight from Egypt. You chose and us You blessed from among all the nations and Your holy Sabbath with love and favor did You give us as a heritage Blessed are You, oh God, who makes holy the Sabbath.

Blessed are You, oh God our lord, king of all creation, who brings forth bread from the earth.

KEEDUSH

קִידוּשׁ

(sing this together)

Barukh atah Adonay,
Blessed are You, oh God
eloheinu melekh ha olam,
our lord, king of all creation
borei pree ha gafen
who creates the fruit of the vine.
Barukh atah Adonay,
Blessed are You, oh God
eloheinu melekh ha olam,
our lord, king of all creation
ah sher keed shahnu bi meetzvotav,
whose commandments make us holy
vi ratza vahnu, vi shabat kadisho
and was pleased with us and with Your Sabbath, which is holy
bi ahava uvratzon heen kheelanu
with love and with favor You gave us as a heritage
zeekaron li ma asei vreisheet
a remembrance of the labor of creation
kee hu yom ti kheela li meekrei
for it is the day that comes before gatherings
kodesh zeikher leetzee at meetz rayim
of holiness in remembrance of the flight from Egypt.
kee vahnu vakharta vi otanu kee dashta
You chose and us You blessed
meekol ha ameem vi shabat kadshi kha
from among all the nations and Your holy Sabbath
bi ahava uvratzon heenkhal tahnu
with love and favor did You give us as a heritage
Barukh atah Adonay,
Blessed are You, oh God,
mi kadeish ha shabat.
who makes holy the Sabbath.

בָּרוּךְ אַתָּה יְיָ
אֱלֹהֵינוּ מֶלֶךְ הָעוֹלָם.
בּוֹרֵא פְּרִי הַגָּפֶן:
בָּרוּךְ אַתָּה יְיָ
אֱלֹהֵינוּ מֶלֶךְ הָעוֹלָם.
אֲשֶׁר קִדְּשָׁנוּ בְּמִצְוֹתָיו
וְרָצָה בָנוּ. וְשַׁבַּת קָדְשׁוֹ
בְּאַהֲבָה וּבְרָצוֹן הִנְחִילָנוּ
זִכָּרוֹן לְמַעֲשֵׂה בְרֵאשִׁית.
כִּי הוּא יוֹם תְּחִלָּה לְמִקְרָאֵי
קֹדֶשׁ זֵכֶר לִיצִיאַת מִצְרָיִם.
כִּי־בָנוּ בָחַרְתָּ וְאוֹתָנוּ קִדַּשְׁתָּ
מִכָּל־הָעַמִּים וְשַׁבַּת קָדְשְׁךָ
בְּאַהֲבָה וּבְרָצוֹן הִנְחַלְתָּנוּ.
בָּרוּךְ אַתָּה יְיָ.
מְקַדֵּשׁ הַשַּׁבָּת:

Barukh atah Adonay, eloheinu melekh
Blessed are You, oh God our lord, king
ha olam, ha motzee lekhem meen ha aretz.
of all creation, who brings forth bread from the earth.

בָּרוּךְ אַתָּה יְיָ אֱלֹהֵינוּ מֶלֶךְ
הָעוֹלָם הַמּוֹצִיא לֶחֶם מִן הָאָרֶץ.

START FROM THE OTHER SIDE
I READ FROM RIGHT TO LEFT